ROOSEVELT

A REVOLUTIONARY WITH COMMON SENSE

by Dr. Helmut Magers

Translated from German by Marianne Farrin

Shady Tree Press
New York, New York

ROOSEVELT, a Revolutionary with common sense was first published in 1933 by R. Kittler Verlag, Leipzig, Germany.

The English version published in 2012 by
Shady Tree Press
136 East 64th Street, 7th Floor
New York, NY 10065

ISBN-13: 978-0-9841211-4-4
ISBN-10: 0-9841211-4-5

Designed by Scribe Freelance
www.scribefreelance.com

Published in the United States of America

ROOSEVELT

A REVOLUTIONARY WITH COMMON SENSE

MARIANNE FARRIN, translator, dedicates her work to her husband, Jim, with thanks for his patience and encouragement throughout.

CONTENTS

Author's Dedication to President Roosevelt   7

FOREWORD: Ambassador William E. Dodd   9

CHAPTER 1:   Roosevelt and the German People   11

CHAPTER 2:   The Will to Win   18

CHAPTER 3:   Hoover's Legacy   49

CHAPTER 4:   Forerunner to the Revolution   60

CHAPTER 5:   The Mood to Experiment   75

CHAPTER 6:   The Dawn of a New Age   89

APPENDIX: a). A Fascist Roosevelt   115
               b). The Key Issue: Youth Pushing   119
                   for Socialism
               c). Bridges to Roosevelt   122

Letters   131

To the President of the United States

Franklin D. Roosevelt

in profound admiration of his
conception of a new economic order
and with devotion to his personality.

The author.

Berlin, Germany, November 9, 1933

FOREWORD
Ambassador William E. Dodd

THE INDUSTRIAL WORLD stretching from the lowlands of Saxony to the hills of Minnesota has for the past three or four years suffered the worst depression in history. Heroic efforts are being made in both Germany and the United States to solve the basic problem of social imbalances, a problem which has not been adequately addressed in the past. Throughout the world it is clear today that self-centered individuals and ruling parties ought not to have unlimited control of government. Input from the finest experts and laypeople together with support of the majority provide the only dependable guiding principle for economic and social leadership.

An extraordinary leader has emerged at the helm of the United States, a person familiar with the history of his country and not representative of any special interest groups. He has the greatest expertise at his disposal and has gathered some of the most intelligent public servants in his administration. I am speaking of President Franklin D. Roosevelt and his staff in Washington who have undertaken the enormous task of restoring the prosperity for everyone which once blessed the land of Benjamin Franklin and Thomas Jefferson.

Dr. Helmut Magers has written a brief and conscientious study of the situation in the United States and the unique leader who has achieved outstanding success already. President Roosevelt and his efforts in Washington ought to be of interest to every educated European and particularly every German, knowing the difficult questions German leaders must also face. Roosevelt has a keen interest in the European questions. He knows that no great country can exist in isolation but that the foundations of any progressive civilization must depend on increased cooperation and a shared peace. I am of the conviction that this careful and sympathetic study by the author will be instructive for many.

BERLIN, OCTOBER 1, 1933.
WILLIAM E. DODD,
U. S. AMBASSADOR TO GERMANY

ONE

Roosevelt and the German People

"WHEN REFORM ARRIVES in America – and it could happen overnight – it will arrive without any revolutionary thunder. We do not shy away from experimentation in America. Once it becomes obvious that the old system can no longer be saved, we might simply try a new system using human intelligence and *common sense*. The time for social reform is long overdue."

These were the words of a keen American observer of his country's political and economic scene. He made this somewhat prophetic statement in the fall of 1931 when political and economic power still rested in the hands of Herbert Hoover for another one and a half years.

I heard this remark with some skepticism. Radical change in America seemed impossible from my point of view. America was still a land of unlimited resources, an enlightened if autocratic capitalism and a completely inadequate trade union movement; in other words, a land that offered no breeding ground for socialist movements. Even the hungry and unemployed citizens remained loyal and did not dream of changing places with their European counterparts. The moderately Socialist Party of Norman Thomas had not been able to date to get a foothold in the country. My question, posed to Norman Thomas of why the difficult economic crisis had not resulted in a political response by the American working class, received a typical explanation. Norman Thomas did not consider the American worker radical but rather as holding on to the hope that, next time, he could withdraw from Wall Street three weeks before another collapse.

To me it seemed like fantasy to speak of a revolution in America. While I could imagine the possibility of social upheaval in every West European country including France, in America civic order appeared as secure as anywhere in the world despite the Depression.

Meanwhile, the United States has become the showcase for a "top-down" revolution that, in generosity and reasoning, surpasses any radical social change currently experienced elsewhere in the world. And it has arrived just like my American friend predicted. The awareness of a bankrupt economic system has led to a new system being tried. The boldness, gamble and strength of the Roosevelt Revolution lie in its experimentation. Despite the enthusiastic support of Roosevelt by the American nation, this does not represent a social movement rising from the ground up. Rather, it is an authoritarian revolution, boldly conceived by a partly-paralyzed individual and promoted by a party as old as the American nation itself.

It is precisely the authoritarian nature of the American Revolution that essentially equates to the German one. Many details in the reform show surprising similarities. The purpose of this small book is to provide insight into the similar developments in the two countries. From such a study a mutually fruitful idea might emerge.

Every new president of the United States is immediately scrutinized on his foreign policy initiatives by the European nations. "Will this president be accommodating on the question of war debts?" debtor nations ask. "Will he be friendly towards the League of Nations and recognize the International Arbitration Tribunal?" Western nations ponder. "Will he be seeing a cradle of peace or the danger of another European war in France?" victor and victims alike question. "Will he be in favor of economic cooperation?" international illusionists try to guess. At the heart of such questions usually lies the hope of economic illusionists of being able to extract American loans. But even more fatal is the delusion of being served such loans. Instead, the question ought merely to be, "Does this president support the Monroe Doctrine if and when it applies to America's involvement in European affairs?"

Statesmen from the Western powers allowed no time to pass before they sought to discern for themselves the position of the new president on these matters. On an immediate departure for the White House, Ramsey MacDonald of Britain came to discuss the World Economic Conference, "economic cooperation" and war debts. The former French President, Eduoard Herriot, likewise arrived in Washington with real political intentions. He was not going to accept anything less than America's agreement to the French "Entente of the Democracies" which could only be interpreted as an aim against the defeated at Versailles.

Despite the cordial visit, MacDonald received an unmistakable answer in America's surrender of the Gold Standard and Roosevelt's reaction to the World Economic Conference. The international illusionists thereby understood that Roosevelt would refuse to join his economic policies with European interests but would simply consider currency and customs issues as they applied to America's own needs.

The French president also gained nothing from Roosevelt. America's rejection of his idea of an Entente of the large Democracies left it up to France to strengthen its own European alliances. After Herriot's return from Washington, Italy, Spain and, last but not least, Russia made noticeable gestures towards such cooperation while Roosevelt in an interview restated his position to a female French journalist: "The United States will never again send a soldier to Europe and will block any nation which deserves a blockade."

In an apparent contradiction, however, the latest news from America comes with America's planned consent to international arms control. It still remains only a tentative agreement but the United States certainly surrenders its earlier position herewith. International arms control in French hands will primarily be directed against Germany and with this consent Roosevelt undoubtedly gives a nod to French politics. However, Roosevelt's instincts still guide him to avoid an American role on the European stage.

It is generally known that Japan is rearming its navy up to the limit of London's Naval Treaty and Japan has announced that under no circumstances will it renew the Naval Treaty expiring at the end of 1935. Instead, Japan will now demand naval parity with England and America. Under such circumstances and within the framework of public jobs creation, Roosevelt likewise intends to rebuild the American Navy up to the limits allowed by the London agreement. Currently, the strength of the American Navy trails these limits by the widest margin. Despite the plans to rebuild the Navy and create jobs, Roosevelt still encounters strong domestic opposition even within his own party.

When, as might have been expected, the Japanese politely and resolutely announced plans to turn down the International Arms Control Treaty, Roosevelt encountered less opposition at home to naval rearmament than previously.

Rebuilding the Navy provides Roosevelt concurrently with an opportunity to pressure America's heavy industries into compliance with the social-political demands of his administration, such as higher wages and a shorter work week.

As far as it is possible to say anything about Roosevelt's foreign policy to date, it is that American foreign policy is slowly shifting its gravitational focus from Europe to the Far East. Japan is seen as the most powerful and active threat to white dominance in the world today and is fast becoming the central focus of the foreign policy interests of the United States. There is not much concern about the Philippines, although the immediate danger remains greater there. Only one hundred kilometers separate the southern-most point of Formosa from the northern-most island of the Philippines. Yet despite the current situation, the Filipinos themselves are staging intense protests after twelve years of waiting and hoping for independence, an independence which the Hoover Administration had wanted to make one of its last official acts.

American interests are much more focused on the many outlying areas of the Pacific Ocean threatened by Japan than on the Philippine Islands. In China as well as in South and Central America attention is focused on the expanding trade policies of the Empire of the Rising Sun and their potential damage to the United States. There is a constant effort in America to recapture ground here. The devaluation of the dollar by fifty percent through an approximate forty percent devaluation of the yen together with the rebuilding of the U.S. Navy are the first signs of a new Pacific orientation in American politics.

A next step in the same direction ought to be America's diplomatic relations with Soviet Russia. Roosevelt has already established the first contact. Long before he assumed office, the former Governor of Wisconsin, Robert La Follette, concluded official talks with the Russians and at the London Conference, Roosevelt's representatives took several opportunities to make contact with the Russian deputies. Such efforts to start diplomatic relations with Russia created more opposition at home than even Roosevelt's naval rearmament. Churches throughout the American provinces launched an especially vigorous campaign against the recognition of the Soviet Union. The following comes from a pamphlet issued by the churches:

> *Communism plays a delicate game. Socialism is the first step towards communism. The line of least opposition leads from the color rose to the color red. America finds itself in the process of a drastic change in governance and a break from our basic foundations. Such changes testify to the truth that public morality is ever sinking deeper.*
>
> *As surely as night follows day, we will experience the demise of our entire social, moral and economic life and, if our citizens do not act quickly, our democratic form of*

government. The handwriting on the wall is disastrous and unequivocal.

The atheistic city of Moscow must be delighted that so many people in high places of our so-called Christian government reach out to their kind. The rumor persists that the Roosevelt Administration is about to start diplomatic relations with Soviet Russia, an aberration which Presidents Wilson, Harding, Coolidge and Hoover refused to be guilty of. The Brain Trust is composed of people whose noses are incapable of perceiving the stench of the Communist refuse. One can hardly expect them to see anything morally despicable in the Red experiment of abolishing all forms of religion.

Here is a press release from Washington, dated June 14, 1933. "We cannot assume it to become common knowledge that the President has finally decided to recognize Soviet Russia. The time for the announcement has not yet been determined. Perhaps he will make it after the adjournment of Congress or at the London Economic Conference."

Concurrent with this announcement, statements in favor of the official recognition of the Soviets will be circulated throughout the country by men such as Senators George Norris and William Borah in an apparent maneuver by the Brain Trust to break the opposition and pave the way for this disastrous alliance. As the Bible says in Isaiah 28:15, "we will have made a contract with hell."

Roosevelt hopes that Japanese stubbornness will remove all current United States obstacles to the recognition of Russia. In the meantime, American cooperation in trade with Russia accelerates. The Reconstruction Finance Corporation, an institute using public funds, apparently finances Russian orders placed in the United States. And as soon as America appoints an ambassador and trade attaché to Moscow, it is safe to count on visible increases in Russian American trade. Already during the last years of the Depression, American exports to Russia held up with noticeable strength. Opposition to Russia was never quite an issue within American financial circles. The iron will with which the Russians seize upon an almost "American-like" building program through a cleverly formulated election slogan, "Speeding up the economy," regularly evokes sympathy in New York. The idea of an American loan to Russia, to support American exports, stop Russian dumping in the United States and to recapture the former market for American agricultural products, surfaces repeatedly. Only great risk stands in the way of such a sizeable loan but such risks are usually passed over to the Federal Government and in the past, the United States has not shied away from undertaking great risks, as for example those undertaken between 1917 and 1920 when America granted loans to Italy, Serbia, Greece, Liberia and Costa Rica.

Acceptance of the Soviet Republic will make the question of a loan to Russia more urgent. Strong participation in such a United States loan authorization can also be expected to carry political weight given the current situation.

Such aspects of American foreign policy are receiving considerable attention in Germany even if Germans are not directly involved in the diplomatic game. But as mentioned before, the focus of American foreign policy today is not centered in Geneva, Paris or even London. It has shifted half way around the world to the Far East.

TWO
The Will to Win

A BIOGRAPHY ON THE childhood of Abraham Lincoln once stated that Lincoln's childhood might be summarized as the short and simple story of poverty. Roosevelt's childhood, on the other hand, is quite a different story. Franklin Delano Roosevelt grew up in the sophisticated atmosphere of wealth. His parents, James R. Roosevelt and Sara Delano, both came from affluent, established New York families. The Roosevelt clan first arrived in the New World from Holland in the 17th century. The Delano family followed shortly thereafter from Flanders, today's Belgium. Franklin Delano Roosevelt was born on January 30, 1882 and spent his childhood on the family's country estate on the Hudson River some one hundred kilometers north of New York City. Here he grew up to become a carefree spontaneous youth amidst the rolling hills, woods and ever flowing Hudson River.

One thing was missing for Franklin: the presence of other children to play with. He was completely dependent on his family for company except for a stepbrother twenty years older. Every year, Franklin was taken on an extended trip to Europe and came to Germany several times where his father sought treatment at Bad Neuheim. While in Germany, Franklin enrolled in summer school and it was here that he improved his comprehension of the German language and he still remembers fondly some of the games he learned while in Germany. But did he come to really comprehend the nature of Europe? Franklin was chauffeured everywhere in the company of his French or German governess and he met few children during such travels. He was unable to play with children different from himself, children who did not speak his language. His unstructured life in the woods, on the water and rivers at home was so much happier. His parents did not send him to the public elementary school in Hyde Park but arranged for a nanny instead and, later, a private tutor to educate their son. The young Franklin primarily learned to ride, swim, fish, sail, and play tennis.

A favorite pastime became jumping in his boat and sailing out to sea. The young man loved the challenge of the water and learned how to handle both sail and wheel in his strong youthful hands. When he peered across the surface of the water and saw an approaching wave, he turned the boat adroitly without losing grip on the sail. By the age of fourteen, he was already an experienced yachtsman. Throughout these years, love of the water was nurtured and stayed with him for the rest of his life. His greatest youthful wish was to become a sailor. Perhaps such love of the sea was inherited from his ancestors. Franklin's maternal great grandfather organized the tea trade with China and had a fleet of sailing ships making frequent journeys around Cape Horn. The young Franklin built ship models at home and when he visits and inspects navy ships as Secretary of the Navy later in life, more experienced naval officers are often surprised by his knowledge of the Navy's many large and sophisticated vessels. And now as president, Roosevelt regularly returns for weekends on the water. Being on the water provided an escape from loneliness during his childhood years. When he could spend an entire afternoon, the wind blowing through his hair, the sail firmly grasped in his hands only to reach the dock countless crossings later, a contented Franklin would sleep soundly that night.

His constant interaction with adults helped Franklin mature early in both mind and spirit. He was not coddled despite the privileged atmosphere at home. When together with other children, Franklin tended to feel superior to them and felt a need to impose his will on others. His mother recalls, "Franklin was determined to control his playmates and he would usually get his way. I once told him, 'My boy, do not always give commands; let other children have their say, too.' 'Mommy,' he answered, 'If I don't give commands they won't do anything.'"

When Franklin turned fourteen, he was sent to Groton, an exclusive school for the sons of the top echelon that is more or less the Eton of the United States. Here he met boys who shared a similar background to his. Franklin was not very popular and made few friends yet played a leading role in the school. Whenever a group formed with a common purpose, Roosevelt desired to be part of that group, and whenever positions requiring group leadership and the exercise of strong will emerged, they usually became his. For example, Franklin became the manager of the school's baseball team, and although he did not play baseball himself, he helped train the team, keep the teammates in shape and act as the final authority in arguments among the players. He also became the Groton baseball strategist, which involved carefully studying the baseball standings of competitive schools, deciding which games Groton ought to play and assuming full responsibility for the school's baseball standings within the New England States.

The yearbooks from Groton show how Roosevelt enjoyed the admiration of his fellow students and how he became a highly respected member of the debate team. There was no subject he could not discuss like an adult. On one hand he would argue for the abolition of the death sentence and on the other, for the modernization of the American naval fleet. At one debate, he might argue for England and the United States to guarantee the safety of China, and at another, leave the strong impression on his classmates that he favored independence for the Philippines with the conviction that the Philippine people would best know how to handle their own freedom.

While at Groton, the spirit of adventure seized him anew. It was the time of the Spanish-American war and Groton students thrilled at the news of war. Roosevelt decided with a friend to march out and enlist. He was seventeen years old. He and his friend

Franklin D. Roosevelt
with his parents.

As manager of the baseball
team at Croton School.

carefully prepared an escape and when their youthful dream of a hero's journey almost became reality, the two young heroes were forced to bed with a high fever the night before their flight. Ironically the doctor's diagnosis of common childhood measles slayed the two prospective young soldiers before they could enter battle.

After Groton, Roosevelt entered Harvard University, one of the oldest and best colleges in the United States. His academic performance at Harvard showed no exceptional promise although he completed his college requirements in three years without any difficulty. Not surprisingly, Roosevelt belonged to the most exclusive clubs at Harvard and was chosen president of his class. Above all, he made a name for himself as the editor of *The Crimson*, the college newspaper that accurately but mercilessly reports on all the various campus activities. It is a paper that also ambitiously tackles the more serious issues of world politics, strives for equality in content with the New York newspapers and at the time, the primary bridge connecting the college community with the outside world. Roosevelt's skillful and courageous reporting primarily focused on college life. He became the respected critic and "big man on campus" because of the sharp wit of his pen. Although he closely followed the interconnections of politics, he held back on political commentary for personal reasons. Roosevelt's cousin five times removed was Theodore R. Roosevelt who was elected President of the United States the same year that Franklin graduated from college.

Franklin continued his education with the study of law at Columbia University. He married Anna Eleanor Roosevelt, a niece of Theodore Roosevelt, in his first year of law school and the two branches of the Roosevelt family were hereby joined. In place of her deceased father, the bride's uncle and American president escorted the bride to the altar and Theodore Roosevelt's daughter, Alice Roosevelt Longworth, was a bridesmaid. She was the young woman who a generation later would campaign and vote for Herbert

Hoover against her Roosevelt cousin.

The career of Franklin Roosevelt showed no special promise for the next several years. His life was first and foremost the journey of a wealthy young man from a privileged background who navigated his way through school with a warmhearted nature. Roosevelt received his law degree in 1907 at the age of twenty-five and accepted a position as attorney with a well-established New York law firm; in 1910 he became active in politics for the first time when he ran as the Democratic candidate for the State Senate of New York and pursued the good will of the electorate of his home district.

Roosevelt's campaign at first seemed totally hopeless. The district had always been overwhelmingly Republican and Roosevelt's Republican opponent was an old respected member of the New York State Senate who had a fiery temperament and who maintained considerable popularity among his constituents. Perhaps Roosevelt's permission to run was only a friendly gesture given to a rich young man in order to maintain the good will of the Democratic Party. But the friends of Roosevelt bet on their candidate to win by a margin of ten to one.

Roosevelt immersed himself in the campaign immediately. He was not a man to pass up a challenge despite the longest odds. He bought a car, still an impressive item at the time, and the car created a sensation wherever he went. Roosevelt visited every village in his district, paid generously for every chicken run over by his car, and stopped to speak at every one of his opponent's campaign stops too. Despite Roosevelt's aristocratic background, he possessed an amazing gift of reaching the hearts of people with whom he was speaking. Each person found him-self personally addressed by Roosevelt and felt that the young man standing before him shared his personal concerns. Roosevelt trumped every new promise of his opponent although that proved to be unnecessary. To everyone's surprise, this time the traditional Republican base voted Democratic and a political novice defeated an old political hand;

Roosevelt became the youngest member to enter the New York State Senate. From each camp malicious whispering was heard that his victory was due to uneducated farmers mistaking Franklin Roosevelt for the son of the great Theodore Roosevelt, totally forgetting that Theodore Roosevelt was a Republican.

Becoming a new senator in the state capital of Albany was not a big prize. An issue of the *Saturday Evening Post* heralded its importance as being somewhere "between a porter and an office assistant." But it did not bother Roosevelt at all to let older and more powerful parliamentarians play a fatherly role with him. The same thing happens in every election to the U. S. Senate from New York. Tammany Hall, the powerful political machine of the New York City Irish, wanted to send a certain William F. Sheehan to Washington when Tammany Hall was at the height of its power. It controlled not only Albany but the entire Democratic machine as well as any legislation throughout the country with far-reaching consequences for the Democrats. Members of both houses of Congress knew a political career must be endorsed by Tammany Hall; no one could oppose them. Even if a candidate did oppose Tammany's domination, such a candidate must still make a declaration of faith and can only give Republicans credit behind closed doors for speaking up about Tammany's corruption. A rebellion against Tammany Hall was equal to political suicide.

Knowing this, Franklin D. Roosevelt, as the new member in Albany, still had the audacity not to support the Tammany candidate, William Sheehan. Upon inquiry, Roosevelt found there was a better candidate for the Senate in Washington and organized an opposition to Tammany Hall. He located eighteen members from both state houses who were neither prominent nor powerful but nevertheless willing to put forth another candidate. And this coalition proved strong enough to hinder the election of William Sheehan.

The head of Tammany Hall, Charles Francis Murphy, became enraged. Roosevelt and the "insurgents" stayed firm. Roosevelt managed to hold them together despite Tammany's attempt to break the insurgency. "I love nothing better than a good fight," he is reported to have said. And this is the same Roosevelt we will encounter later as well.

Tammany's unceasing pressure on these elected officials proved unable to break their resolve. The New York State Assembly was furious with the young Roosevelt and his obstinate desire to impose his own will. Republicans and Democrats both pushed him repeatedly and with much displeasure and anxiety caused waves in Albany. But new voices surfaced among the voters who welcomed the fight against Tammany and who lent their support to the young challenger, Roosevelt. Across the state of New York a crisis loomed. Murphy, head of Tammany Hall, finally condescended to call Roosevelt to a conference in New York where Roosevelt achieved a victory. Tammany Hall would let its candidate, William Sheehan, lose as long as Roosevelt's candidate did not get nominated and together they agreed on the support of an unblemished third person, James O'Gorman.

The election became a victory of David over Goliath. For the first time, Tammany Hall lost both its power and reputation and declined in influence as a direct result of this fight with Roosevelt. Choosing a U. S. senator became not simply a fight of one stubborn personality against an enormously entrenched power, but carried deeper political significance. After Roosevelt's confrontation with Tammany, a new movement emerged which finally divested Albany of its right to choose New York Senate candidates for Washington and this right returned to the people of New York.

Tammany Hall sought revenge on the recalcitrant young Roosevelt. He would have to pay for such brazenness and for going against the wisdom of those more experienced at the start of a political career. The election must be interpreted as only a chance happening or at least, simply a mistake. A public announcement was made. None of the eighteen insurgents who joined Roosevelt would return to the state legislature in the next election. And in fact, only Franklin D. Roosevelt does.

At the end of his first term in Albany, Roosevelt was well known throughout the state of New York. During his second term in the State Senate, Roosevelt initiated another confrontation with Tammany Hall. Roosevelt, an early supporter of Governor Woodrow Wilson for president preaching the benefits of what he calls "The New Freedom," attached himself to the Woodrow Wilson platform. "No one can deny," Wilson proclaimed, "that the place for private initiative has grown scarce and more difficult. No one aware of the industrial development of our country can deny that credit is ever more difficult to find and obtained only through self-effort and the interchange with those who run the country's industries. And finally, no one can deny that when someone tries to compete with an industrial complex existing on the largesse of enormous capital powers, individuals eventually are forced to sell or close out."

Roosevelt participated in the 1912 Democratic Party Convention in Baltimore in 1912. Wilson's candidacy was put forth without the endorsement of Tammany Hall. Roosevelt threw himself into the Wilson presidential campaign and promoted him at dozens of campaign stops. And following Wilson's victory, the new president promoted his enthusiastic supporter to Assistant Secretary of the Navy and Secretary of the Marine Corps. This was how Roosevelt started the next chapter of his life. From the backwater corridors of Albany he arrived in Washington at a critical juncture to take up two responsible positions in the nation's capital, rapidly becoming the center of world politics.

The new position was ideal for Roosevelt. The ocean had always been as life giving for him as the solid ground of the earth. He had compiled over the span of years a whole library on shipping and oceanography, and was the owner a noteworthy collection of ship models which he had started building in childhood. Even during his time as a lawyer in New York City, Roosevelt worked on many cases involving merchant vessels and accidents at sea. Now, to the delight of New York Democrats, he happily exchanged a senate seat in Albany for this new position as Assistant Secretary of the Navy.

An approaching world war was already in the air and Roosevelt became the enthusiastic proponent of the "readiness principle." He studied the preparedness of the Navy and reorganized the bases along the U. S. coastline. Navy ports were refurbished, new weapons ordered and the fleet modernized. He worked without consulting Congress and initiated several projects before Congress had even authorized them. In this rearming of the Navy, Roosevelt often encountered obstacles and belated approvals by Congress, but nevertheless managed to push the work forward. Members of Congress became aware of the enormous spread of wharfs, docks and industries stretching for thousands of miles along the American coastline, while the actual Navy had hardly seen any growth for years. But when war broke out, Roosevelt's Department of the Navy was prepared. More than one hundred thousand dockworkers were called into service and the fleet was ready within a short time to face any navy it might meet in battle. Readiness for wartime production followed without any organizational adjustment.

Roosevelt became one of the most important personalities in the Wilson Cabinet during those years. Foreign embassies sought his friendship. An especially strong genuine friendship developed between the English Ambassador, Sir Cecil Spring-Rice, and the Roosevelt family. Likewise, the French Ambassador, Jean Jules Jusserand, often also appeared at the Roosevelt home and the Roosevelt clan's fluency in French made him feel at home. Not coincidentally, Roosevelt had his pulse on all aspects of foreign policy during these years. The Departments of Navy and State shared the same building in Washington and daily interactions between the top officials in both departments became commonplace.

When the English-French High Commission arrived in Washington, it was Roosevelt who served as the special escort for the allied diplomats. President Wilson allowed himself to be persuaded by Roosevelt's negotiations with John Balfour and Rene Viviani. And when Roosevelt arrived in Europe in July 1918 as Wilson's personal representative for direct talks on the continuation of the war with the Allies, it was Roosevelt at Versailles who was the most well known personality in the American delegation, apart from President Woodrow Wilson and Colonel Edward M. House.

The absolute will to win remained a strong characteristic of the Roosevelt personality and this trait animated him throughout the war. The famous barricade in the North Sea of three rows of vessels even including fishing boats, enforced in 1917 by the Norwegians between Scotland and Norway, practically paralyzed the German U-boat fleet and was essentially Roosevelt's idea. The British Admiralty dismissed such a plan as unenforceable, but Roosevelt executed the barricade nevertheless. He became an extreme militarist during those years. At the same time, he remained the most loyal confidante of Woodrow Wilson and embraced the President's ideals with almost missionary zeal. Even today Roosevelt acknowledges the following:

In 1920, millions of fellow Americans and I supported in word and deed America's participation in a League of Nations, a community of nations born of the highest ideal and meant to carry the important banner which calls for the prevention of another world war. I do not want to excuse such zeal but today, the League of Nations is not the same League as Woodrow Wilson first envisioned; in the intervening years it has failed to move in the direction envisioned by its founder. Instead, important members of the League are in no way disposed to cut their enormous sums spent on armaments or to channel these same large sums into credit for legitimate trade, balanced budgets and the payments of debt.

Roosevelt remained true to Wilson's ideals even after Congress stopped cheering "Hosanna" and instead changed the battle cry to "Crucify him." Roosevelt frequently still uses Wilson phraseology even though Wilson's influence on Roosevelt seems to have been mainly indirect. One might think one still hears Wilson when the following words on governance are heard: "To govern implies being able to formulate a political agenda and using the political process, to bring desired results as long as these have the support of the general public. To govern essentially means to persuade, lead, sacrifice and continually inform the public for perhaps the greatest duty of the statesman is to teach the people." Yet, these words are not those of Wilson, but Roosevelt's own.

After the war, Roosevelt's military mindset transformed itself quickly to enthusiastically support every effort to maintain a lasting peace. At the Conference in Washington in 1921, Roosevelt became personally involved in setting restrictions on naval armaments and, at Geneva in 1927 and London in 1930 he participated actively in the negotiations for an armaments freeze. The American Relief Response to Germany and Austria during Versailles in 1919 also came to fruition as a result of Roosevelt's efforts.

His eight years in Washington with the Department of the Navy increased Roosevelt's strong personal reputation, and his unwavering support for Wilson no longer became an issue, despite the Democratic Party's complete abandonment of its former President. At the Democratic Convention in 1920, James M. Cox received the nomination for president while Roosevelt nominated his loyal supporter, Woodrow Wilson, instead. Such a contrarian position brought unexpected results. The Governor of New York, Alfred E. Smith and later also a candidate for president, rose to nominate the constant lone ranger, Franklin D. Roosevelt, for vice president. And with loud acclamation the thirty-eight year old Roosevelt became the Democratic ticket's vice-presidential candidate.

Roosevelt approached the national election with the same

commitment he had approached all previous fights. He traveled throughout the United States and everywhere challenged listeners with his personality and power of oratory. The election broke all records. Roosevelt made more than 800 campaign speeches and traveled to every one of the forty-eight states, crisscrossing the country. He remained true to Wilson's ideology and to America's entry into the League of Nations. His partner in the Democratic fight for president, James Cox, joined him along with the dying President Wilson, and Roosevelt persuaded Cox to adopt Wilson's ideals. The two candidates advocated for an international foreign policy for the United States and for America's entry into the League of Nations. But on the day of the election, the people chose the Republican candidate instead. President Wilson learned firsthand during his two four-year terms as president that treaties of war and peace do not receive the approval of the American people. Warren G. Harding, the Republican candidate, promised both the right and left that the time had come for the country to return to "normal days" and was chosen by the electorate instead of the Democratic ticket. The Republicans once again steered the ship of state.

Following the defeat, which Roosevelt interpreted as a defeat of Woodrow Wilson's policies, Roosevelt returned to his private law practice. This defeat, however, became the most difficult disappointment in Roosevelt's life to date. The work of his mentor and champion had not yet been fulfilled; an enemy had caused its collapse. Roosevelt believed himself to be finished with politics, the tide finally having turned against him and leaving him no alternative but to rethink and regroup.

Immediately following his retreat, a terrible fate struck Roosevelt. The year was 1921. Roosevelt took a short vacation in August to drive his family north to the coast of Canada where they owned a small summer cottage. He felt carefree and burden-free at last. Roosevelt plunged into the frigid ocean for a refreshing swim but returned home chilled, woke up the next morning with a fever and strange symptoms and stayed in bed, unable to explain what ailed him. The idea of being sick was unacceptable to a man as fit as Roosevelt and he considered the illness nothing to worry about. However, when he tried to get out of bed, his legs refused to cooperate. Able to lift his upper body, the legs still remained immobile. The local doctor contacted a specialist in New York who suggested it might be an attack of polio and arranged for Roosevelt's immediate transfer to New York.

Suddenly, the thirty-nine-year-old with a promising political career lay bedridden and paralyzed, and forced under the best of circumstances to await an uncertain future in a wheelchair. Political opponents silently gloated even when they expressed their sympathy for the personal misfortune of this fearless politician. The symptoms of the illness slowly disappeared but the legs refused to cooperate and remained immobile.

Roosevelt wanted to know the truth about his condition and when he suspected not being told the truth by his relatives, he dispatched Louis McHenry Howe, his personal secretary, friend and a frequent houseguest of the Roosevelt family, to see Professor Robert Lovett, the attending physician.

Doctor Lovett gave Howe a carefully veiled message lest he further depress the patient. According to Doctor Lovett, polio was rare for a man of Roosevelt's age and therefore it would be hard to predict the next phase of the disease. But this much the doctor could say for certain: if Roosevelt's condition did not deteriorate further, there might still be some hope for some improvement, but certainly never a return to his unusual energy and tenacity. It would require hours, days, weeks, months and yes, even years of constant exercise to rework the muscles. Such exercises must be undertaken daily. However, if the patient had a will strong enough to stay active, there was always a chance of improvement over a course of years.

Howe brought Roosevelt the doctor's unfiltered words. "Very good, then," was Roosevelt's only response. "When will the exercises begin? What will I have to do?" The serum used today on polio patients had not yet been discovered, but awareness of it stirs enough interest in Roosevelt and he becomes one of the first to donate blood for the manufacture of the serum. As a result, a child afflicted with polio is treated with Roosevelt's blood.

Mr. Howe described Roosevelt's heroic fight towards recovery thus, "I have seen him concentrating in bed with such determination that just the movement of his big toe literally made perspiration run down his face. Not once did he stop his exercises during the first three or four critical years and whenever the exertion became too strenuous, he saw it as yet another challenge to overcome. A year or so after he first got polio, I surprised him one morning when I entered and saw him raise and lower his foot, turn it from right to left and with youthful vigor shout, 'People cannot possibly understand how happy it makes me feel to simply wriggle my foot.' I cannot remember him ever complaining or avoiding the strenuous discipline he imposed on himself."

Only a few continued their friendship with the erstwhile, enormously popular politician during those early years of paralysis. To most of the world, Roosevelt became nothing but a paralyzed man and politician irrelevant to politics. Roosevelt's mind however, stayed vitally alert during his absence from the world. He read more than he had ever read before and contemplated thoroughly the problems of governance and politics. The endless diversions of an active life no longer pulled him away. Instead, his hunger for life's meaning grew exponentially during the long years of convalescence. He learned how to use his illness in the most personally fruitful way and allowed no room for distractions. Roosevelt with his familiar determination concentrated on the physical body and on the mind and, in the process, increased his knowledge of both country and economics. In talking with the few friends who stayed loyal, the first "brain trust" emerged to become the foundation for important later reforms that Roosevelt would in due time put into effect as Governor of New York.

The Roosevelt home in Hyde Park, New York

By 1924, Roosevelt yearned for the political stage once more. The Democratic Party was holding its Convention at Madison Square Garden in New York. The usual arguments over who should be the Democratic candidate for president resurfaced. A familiar face appeared at the podium, a politician whom all the elders of the party had already dismissed as irrelevant. This man was Roosevelt. He entered to nominate Alfred E. Smith for president. The resurrected Roosevelt received an overwhelming ovation despite the fact that his candidate failed to be chosen. Four more years would pass before the party nominated Alfred E. Smith.

Roosevelt returned to his law practice on crutches. He asked to retire from the firm but his friends would not accept his resignation. As a result, he traveled to the office daily to attend to his duties. The crutches, steel braces and thin legs were ignored wherever he went and Roosevelt quickly dismissed all expressions of sympathy. He refused questions about his sufferings even from his best friends and never referred to the subject. And yet, thoughts on how to reemerge were continually on his mind. He was certainly able to manage on crutches without a wheelchair, but definitely wanted to overcome even this handicap. Unable to drive, shift gears, brake and use his foot on the gas pedal made Roosevelt dependent on a chauffeur to drive him to the office and marked him as a cripple. The affliction had only been half-way beaten; Roosevelt would never fully recover, but tried to relegate the handicap to as insignificant a place as possible. Roosevelt determined to live and not be disabled. He would lock the disability in a tiny box, contain it and begin his second offensive against the paralysis.

In the fall of 1924, three years after first contracting polio, a friend and well-known benefactor, George Foster Peabody of Boston, told Roosevelt about a small unknown health spa in Georgia with warm springs. The water with relatively high temperatures is supposed to come from a deep spring and have special healing properties. In the past, Indians seemed to have been cured by these waters. It is called Warm Springs and Roosevelt determined to winter and to fight his polio there. He donned a bathing suit and allowed a guard to carry him into the warm waters. Then, an exercise routine began. Roosevelt slowly tried to bend his knees and to straighten them again.

Gradually the stiff limbs responded to the hot springs and hints of life returned to his muscles. Hour after hour, day after day, Roosevelt hung suspended in the water by a life vest under his arms. A few weeks later, he actually began to move his legs up and down, treading water. And it was not long before he was walking on land once more. In approaching the shore, Roosevelt sought the ground under his feet and when he found his footing, slowly moved onto the shore. First, the shoulders lifted him; the chest emerged from the water and, placing one foot in front of the other, gradually the legs carried the heavy weight resting upon them. Roosevelt tried every day to come closer to shore. With every step of progress, a victorious smile returned to Roosevelt's face, the famous FDR smile later to capture a nation.

Roosevelt left Warm Springs after a few months. He now walked with two walking sticks and no longer needed the crutches. The following winter, he returned to Warm Springs. At the end of the treatment, Roosevelt was able to drive his car and even to mount horses. For him, doubt no longer existed that he would conquer his paralysis. Roosevelt returned regularly every winter for a few weeks and because of Roosevelt's money and reputation, this relatively unknown little place became a famous healing spa for those afflicted with polio. Many found their condition improved at Warm Springs.

In 1927, Roosevelt established the Georgia Warm Springs Foundation with funds to bring the spa up to modern standards. Subsequently, famous millionaires donated large sums of money to the Georgia Warm Springs Foundation too, and according to Roosevelt's will, the Sanatorium and Health Spa of Warm Springs was established as a not-for-profit institution. "The common good" became its guiding principle with capitalism's "drive for profit" strictly forbidden. Later as Governor of New York, Roosevelt enforced the same principle in establishing the public baths at Saratoga Springs. The State was not to be in business in the area of healing spas. The Spa at Saratoga Springs must only charge one dollar per person. As a result, largely the sick from the middle class come to Saratoga Springs while the upper class reserves Saratoga Springs only for the Annual Horse Race. Wealthy Americans still seek out private European health spas instead.

Professor and well known German specialist in warm water cures, Doctor Paul Haertl from the State Laboratory of Scientific Research in Healing Springs at Bad Kissingen, received an important role in the expansion of Warm Springs. It was developed partly according his plans. Roosevelt repeatedly invited Dr. Haertl to the United States and, as the only foreigner, appointed him a consulting specialist on the Board of Directors of the Georgia Warm Springs Foundation. It might be said that as a result of Roosevelt's illness, an enormous interest in spring-water cures developed in the United States. It became Roosevelt's cherished idea to establish an international academy in New York for the scientific research of health spas in collaboration with German scholars.

Thanks to the regular cures at Warm Springs, Roosevelt learned to walk sprightly without noticeable difficulty as long as someone lent him an arm and his walking stick was in the other hand. Roosevelt was convinced that he absolutely would learn to move like a normal individual again. He was now able to stand without help, support himself with the arms on a table, and give lengthy speeches without outside aid.

During the most recent campaign, Roosevelt had an accident while giving a speech. As he was emphasizing an important point, Roosevelt leaned forward with his arms to demonstrate the meaning when he lost his balance and stumbled to the utter dismay of the audience. People rushed to Roosevelt, bent over him to straighten the large robust figure again. But Roosevelt wanted to go back to the podium; he gratefully freed himself from the helpers and continued the speech at exactly the point where he fell forward. The crowd gave him an enormous ovation. It might be said that his disability and the energy with which he minimized it greatly added to his popularity. His handicap became legendary and it carried its own symbolic meaning when the United States in 1932 chose a cripple as President, a man who had conquered personal affliction.

The American people were so grounded that, in spite of severe poverty, complaints about circumstances were strictly forbidden whereas conquests over adversity and triumphs of health captured the public's imagination. For that reason, misfortune brought a dividend to Roosevelt and paralysis became an essential part of who he was. He had personal familiarity with the adversities of life. Before becoming paralyzed, Roosevelt exclusively traveled among the elites of the world. Even though the upper classes of the New World were historically more connected with the common man than their European counterparts, and even though Roosevelt was highly esteemed by all subordinates and in the past, as Secretary of the Navy, showed special understanding for the misfortunes of laid-off shipyard workers, he first became a real advocate for the "forgotten man" after his own meeting with destiny. As a cripple he had been pushed to the depths of existence. Al Smith's former advantage with the public as a son of Irish immigrants and earlier, a New York newspaper boy, was surpassed by Roosevelt in his struggle with the misfortunes of polio.

Up until 1928, Roosevelt stayed adamant in refusing a return to political life. He rejected every opportunity, whether a senate seat from New York or the governorship of the state. Roosevelt explained repeatedly that he owed it to his family to continue to work on improving his physical health. But in 1928, the New York Democrats failed to find agreement on a candidate for governor. The convention turned into a terrible circus of dissent. Al Smith, the former governor and leader of the New York Democrats, reached despairingly for the telephone and placed a long distance call to Warm Springs. He pled with Roosevelt to head the Democratic ticket. Roosevelt refused again. Smith persisted and appealed to Roosevelt's friendship. Roosevelt repeated his "No." Finally in a softer, more reproachful voice Smith asked, "And if the convention still nominates you, will you consider being a candidate?" Roosevelt remained silent. Smith returned to the convention to announce that Roosevelt will run.

With Roosevelt as their candidate the Democrats gained an unexpectedly huge victory in New York. But Smith, in campaigning for the presidency, lost the state, whereas Roosevelt won the governorship by a large majority. One Democrat was defeated and another one victorious. All eyes now focused on the man who had succeeded in winning more votes even than the popular Al Smith.

Al Smith greeted his successor in Albany as "Frank." But the situation soon changed and differences emerged. The old conflict between Roosevelt and Tammany Hall flared up again. The Democrats favored laws that Roosevelt singlehandedly rejected and the Republicans enjoyed the opponents' domestic infighting. The past friendship of Roosevelt and Al Smith broke apart. But Roosevelt knew how to garner a stronger ally, the public.

The main battle in Albany centered on the exploitation of electric power from the St. Lawrence River. While in office the former Governor Smith did not champion a state-run electric facility, but lobbied for energy to be distributed among private electric companies. An enormous potential disadvantage for the consumer rested therein. It is not enough to produce cheap electricity if it cannot be delivered cheaply also. The Republicans remained unified in their conservative position: keep the situation as is; a publicly-run electric facility is difficult to justify on conservative principles. Roosevelt insisted, however, on keeping the consumer from being overcharged. The state must be the one to build the overland cables and to sell the electricity back to the people of New York.

Roosevelt's position represented a break with the sacred principles of private enterprise. The state would "step into business" and would be in competition with the private sector. The Republicans mounted a firestorm against such abandonment of the sacred American tradition while Roosevelt calmly rebutted them. "Industrial suppliers shall not be our masters but our servants." In the heated debates that followed, the public attacked the opposition and registered an overwhelming majority on Roosevelt's side.

This took place in 1930, the first year of the Depression when everyone still believed things would soon look up again. New York Democrats and Tammany Hall came under public pressure to re-nominate Roosevelt for governor. In every New York election one inexhaustible subject for discussion between Democrats and Republicans was the subject of welfare agencies. Roosevelt won by a majority of 725,000 votes, the largest majority of any party ever in the history of New York State.

During his second term as governor, Roosevelt enjoyed a Democratic majority in both state houses as well. The Republicans were hopelessly pushed on the defensive. Roosevelt became the red flag, the radical, the socialist, and Republicans knew that Roosevelt could only be defeated if they enflamed his opposition to Tammany Hall. It was most effectively done by drawing him into the dirty politics of the City Council of New York. New corruption charges against New York Mayor Jimmy Walker were repeatedly brought to Roosevelt's attention. Tempt Roosevelt and lure him down a precipice. Roosevelt, however, maintained his cool and did not exceed his area of responsibility. With more serious concerns on his plate, he deftly navigated his way through the Republican obstacles by maintaining a strictly loyal posture.

Tammany Hall feared the paws of the lion and turned ever more hostile towards Roosevelt. Roosevelt's friends, too, were frustrated by his "mild" responses to the New York scandals. "The Evening World" newspaper tweaked his lame backbone of heroism further. "With Tammany's hostility, Governor Roosevelt could lose the next election and still be a good leader. But instead, he has lost his reputation which no victory can make up to him."

In the next election, however, Roosevelt campaigned not for governor but for the presidency of the United States. When the final votes of the National Democratic Convention were counted, only thirty-one of the ninety-four New York State delegates cast their vote for Roosevelt; the majority went to Al Smith. Roosevelt's reputation outside the borders of New York State was responsible for his overwhelming convention victory.

The Democratic National Convention in Chicago in June, 1932, presented a picture of great confusion. The convention lacked leadership. It lacked the authority of a foreordained candidate. Many groups plotted against each other. Furthermore, temperatures were hot and delegates suffered from thirst. They stayed mainly in the corridors where politics were negotiated on a more informal basis. Everyone was loud and screaming in a state of confusion. No one listened to the longwinded deliberations no matter how reasonable they were. Yet despite the terrible circumstances, issues had to be dealt with. When times are difficult, the wise among the Democrats rise to blossom. President Hoover, the most unpopular man in America, was at the end of his term yet the Republicans were unable to replace him and must allow him to campaign once more. Whenever the picture of President Hoover appeared in weekly newsreels at even the smallest local cinemas across the nation, a tumultuous chorus of catcalls regularly exploded. Already as early as March, 1932, a mayor from a Chicago suburb made the following public plea, "I beg all residents of this town to remember that Mr. Hoover is the President of the United States. Therefore, withhold all disrespectful demonstrations when the President's picture appears on the screen. Anyone who boos Mr. Hoover boos his country and thus himself as well."

Under these circumstances the Democratic candidate fared better in 1932 than in 1928. Al Smith wanted to run for president again and relied heavily on his following in New York. But Southern and Western Democrats turned against Al Smith. The West mistrusted him because he was a Catholic and the South rejected him because he was born in Ireland and thus not "one hundred percent American." Western Democrats wanted to raise the banner of William McAdoo and the South the banner of Albert Richie, Governor of Maryland. There was no consensus on a candidate and here was the chance for Roosevelt's friends to lobby for Roosevelt.

James Farley, who led the deliberations, did not make a big speech but behind the scenes pitted the Western delegates against each other so that McAdoo had no chance to survive. If they wanted to beat Smith they must choose Roosevelt. Roosevelt, too, had many friends in New York and he was a Protestant. Farley heard more or less the same thing from the Southern delegates who only added that in contrast to Smith, Roosevelt was one hundred percent American. Finally, Farley spoke personally to the supporters of Smith to show them how slim Smith's chances were when considering the opposition from the West and South and Farley suggested that the wisest thing was to elect his friend, Roosevelt, essentially as liberal a candidate as Smith and one who would proceed with a politics akin to the spirit of Smith.

The plan worked splendidly. When Roosevelt's name was brought before the convention, a huge majority from every sector of the country rallied behind him and his home state of New York became the only one to deny him its allegiance.

Al Smith left the convention, sick, distraught and with a deep personal grievance against Roosevelt. McAdoo was delighted with Smith's defeat and the friends of Roosevelt now took the convention into their own hands. Everything became organized. Roosevelt arrived by plane from Albany for a rousing speech to infuse the convention with new life. Roosevelt announced his support for the abolition of Prohibition and presented a detailed program for rebuilding the economy. Roosevelt saw the root of evil in the farm problem and outlined measures to forgive and bring tax relief to farmers while at the same time lift the price of grain. His plans were based on Roosevelt's past experience with agriculture in New York State. Roosevelt highlighted his experiences as governor of New York and, despite the hostility from his own constituency, proposed an extension of public control of the economy. He wanted to bring agencies such as banks, stock and commodity exchanges under the influence of the government. Every kind of social insurance for the unemployed must be enacted as well.

The entire program was ironclad. His opponents would be able to label Roosevelt as a socialist or radical but Roosevelt knew what the country needed in this time of distress and what side the American people were on. For a long time, no Democratic program had carried so clear a mandate and no party convention had presented so clear and uniform a picture as the one that emerged when Roosevelt seized control.

Roosevelt started to campaign immediately and journeyed by special train with his wife, children, doctor, secretary and the chief of the Brain Trust, Professor Thomas Moley. Roosevelt understood how to relate to his listeners. The winning smile was flashed everywhere. He summoned his wife and children onto the platform of the train or put himself in the midst of a crowd so that farmers could finally feel that they were part of a big family occasion. There was no doubt about his victory among the people. But it was not just a personal touch that gave the campaign such a glow. It was also the fact that Roosevelt understood how to offer more than the tired, oft-repeated campaign slogans.

Whenever Roosevelt addressed the farmers, his favorite topic became how to fight the agricultural crisis. But as a fellow landowner who had experimented on his own fields, Roosevelt also knew what he was talking about. Furthermore, he had worked out and implemented certain features of basic farm support already in the State of New York. When speaking in the cities, Roosevelt addressed the pressing issues of social security and extension of state control over business affairs. Roosevelt did not speak from any specific ideological standpoint but from actual experience and his talks were based on facts and knowledge. Professor Moley supplied the necessary background material during the campaign trail.

Roosevelt by no means had an easy time everywhere. Throughout the country Democrats held different positions on various subjects and Roosevelt's agenda of reform received no unanimous applause. Overall, however, Roosevelt managed to win large personal audiences even when his ideas were not universally embraced. He had his own tried and true methods. In several Mid-Western and Western states there were U.S. senators who called themselves Republicans but who stood in opposition to many of Hoover's policies. This was true of Robert La Follette's brother in Wisconsin, Senator George Norris of Nebraska, Senator Hiram Johnson of California, Senator William Edgar Borah and others.

In the states of these senators Roosevelt would usually start a campaign speech by detailing the work of such Republican servants in Washington and by praising their contributions to the heavens with the result that people believed Roosevelt to be honoring his opponents and that these senators with raised banners, too, were defecting to Roosevelt's camp.

Roosevelt's first grand tour left the country with the impression that the election was already decided. President Hoover continued in the White House allowing the Republican Party and his cabinet to conduct the campaign for him. Hoover wanted to signal that he remained responsible to his presidential duties with time left over for campaigning once or perhaps twice. And Hoover held on to the premise, "Give me a bull market of ten percent and I will be reelected." The market did return briefly, but the upswing was based on uncertain variables and did not hold until November. The resulting stock market collapse caused new stock market lows.

War veterans gathered to demonstrate in the Capital and to demand a pension but when their camp was set on fire, the public, rightly or wrongly, blamed President Hoover and his dministration.

A weak government finally became energized but the energy brought disastrous results. The general election started in Maine a few months earlier than in the rest of the country and Maine voted Democratic despite it being a Republican stronghold.

Hoover finally woke up. Something must happen. Like Roosevelt, he equipped a special train and started a campaign journey surrounded by security. It was autumn. The leaves were already covering White House lawns when the President started campaigning. In the wide open regions of the Midwest, Hoover faced a constant rain that never let up. An organized campaign event in Kansas City was attended by staunch Republicans and came off without incident but even the applause extended at the end was programmed. Hoover hoped for an opportunity to change the mood of his campaign. But when Hoover stood in front of farmers in Des Moines, Iowa, he realized how great Roosevelt's lead already was. Hoover decided to unveil his most powerful weapon. He spoke about the terrible international state of the dollar and in heroic words described his administration's efforts to preserve the stability of the currency. But instead of applause, Hoover received only a few disgruntled responses. Then Owen D. Young of New York stepped forward to present some immediate currency-related measures, but the damage was done. Hoover's admission to the weakness of the dollar triggered a slump on the international currency exchanges and the domestic market followed. The American voters became afraid and angry with their President.

Roosevelt's personal charm won him much sympathy, a sympathy which totally escaped President Hoover. A smile did not represent Hoover's personality. Therefore, Mrs. Hoover was forced to smile all the more and photographers repeatedly raised their flash guns when Mrs. Hoover stood next to her husband on the campaign train, smiling. On one occasion, a clumsy photographer dropped a magnesium bulb on the platform by mistake. It shattered with a loud noise. Mrs. Hoover screamed with a piercing cry and called for an attendant. She summoned the photographers and reporters to her

Roosevelt campaigning.

Roosevelt campaigning.

special railroad car, gave them a stern lecture and asked them to pick up the pieces so that no child would be injured thereby. The story made the headlines in all the American newspapers and no one trusted Mrs. Hoover's smile again.

Roosevelt, on the other hand, traveled the entire country without tiring. No sooner did he return to New York from a round trip than he started another to regions not yet visited. If he lingered in a region with similar economic infrastructures, he repeated the same speech every day. Morley complained, "Governor, hopefully today we might hear something new." "Absolutely not," Roosevelt chuckled. "Nothing pleases people more than to hear a familiar song."

Roosevelt's campaign was one long victory train. The Republicans sensed their chances slipping away. If unable in the last hours to make the voters afraid of Roosevelt through personal vilification, then a Democratic victory was guaranteed. They again tried the same personal defamation that proved effective in the 1928 campaign against Al Smith. In 1928, thousands of wagging tongues like whispers carried innuendoes from place to place and were now recalled – "Al Smith in the White House? That means America will become a State of the Pope – Don't you realize? – Al Smith has already prepared an invitation for the Pope to move to Washington from Rome – It comes from most reliable sources – Don't you understand yet? – The New York scandals and Al Smith! – And imagine Mrs. Smith in the White House."

Thousands of tongues were now set in motion again. Roosevelt is an opportunist, a shifty risk taker without a clear program. Even from the Republican family of Theodore Roosevelt, the other branch of the Roosevelt family, rumors circulated that Franklin Delano is not a true Roosevelt; he does not have the fire of the Roosevelt clan. He is a man without the qualifications for high office, an opportunist who wants to be president. Roosevelt will mean unending disaster for the United States, a postponement of the financial crisis for many years, and nothing but difficult setbacks and chaos.

Roosevelt's friends took the high road and exposed Wall Street as the instigator of these insidious rumors. After all, Wall Street had reason to be nervous about Roosevelt. But it became the best publicity for him. If Wall Street attacks Roosevelt, he must be a man of the people.

Finally, in the last few weeks before the election, Al Smith and Roosevelt reconciled with each other. With the election of Governor Herbert H. Lehmann of New York, two old friends face Tammany Hall together. In the last weeks of the campaign, Al Smith even stumped on the campaign trail for Roosevelt and brought on board his own supporters from the populous New England states. Roosevelt's victory was secured. Hoover, on the other hand, received only the somewhat weak and limited support of ex-President Calvin Coolidge as well as the indisputable support of leading entrepreneurs. Shortly before the election, Henry Ford sent an unsolicited memo from Management Headquarters at River Rouge Works in Detroit to his considerable power base of workers, employees and owners of Ford garages across the country; in other words everyone directly or indirectly associated with Ford. It reads as follows:

> *President Hoover has defeated powers which might have destroyed all industry and work. His efforts to bring employment back are starting to show results. We remain convinced that any deviation from the Hoover program will be disastrous for industry and employment. President Hoover must be reelected in order to prevent the times from getting worse and to make sure they get better. This is our conviction and we forward this memo to all Ford employees and their families throughout the country for their sober awakening.*

Despite these efforts, the battle was lost. Straw polls from political pundits correctly forecast Hoover's defeat. The only surprise on November 8, 1932, is the extent of Roosevelt's victory. Roosevelt receives the biggest majority of any American president in the history of the United States. He triumphs over Hoover with twenty-five and a half million votes, while Hoover is barely able to count sixteen million. Except for the states of Connecticut, Delaware, Maine, New Hampshire, Pennsylvania and Vermont, Roosevelt wins forty-two states. Four hundred and seventy-two electoral votes go to Roosevelt and only fifty to Hoover. The election is indeed a landslide. A few hours after the first results are made known President Hoover sends congratulations to Roosevelt from his place in Palo Alto, California, where without appetite and without friends he has spent the Election Day alone. The country accepts the wide margin of the election and the people hope not to be disappointed by the new president who has promised them so much.

THREE

The Hoover Legacy

"Prosperity is not an empty word. It implies work for everyone. It means security and protection for every business and every home. Policies of the Republican Party aim to join basic necessity with progress for the wider expansion of this prosperity."

—HERBERT HOOVER,
October 1928

IT IS BITTER INJUSTICE that the political and social make-up known as the Hoover Legacy became Roosevelt's inheritance on Inauguration Day, March 4, 1933. Hoover was as innocent of the economic collapse as Harding and Coolidge were not responsible for the fantastic growth of American prosperity in the years leading up to 1929. So when Hoover's legacy is spoken of here it is meant only in a generic sense and not in the sense of someone's last will and testament.

Hoover's legacy is that of the liberal *night watchman state* as it has existed in pure classical form in the United States alone. Such a state fundamentally refuses to intervene in the life of business and that premise corresponds with the American view of government. As a result, no social legislation comes under the jurisdiction of the federal government but belongs to the individual states and nowhere in the civilized world is social legislation as backward as in the United States. Women's and children's labor has been sufficiently protected in only a few American states and so far nothing has been uttered concerning the average workday or social security. Therefore a twelve-hour day is not a rarity but the norm in Southern textile mills. The production procedures, instituted by Henry Ford, account for only a small slice of American industry. It is estimated that only twenty percent of American companies are organized on the capitalist model of Henry Ford. The principles of unrestricted freedom have led to an irresponsible exploitation of the weakest members of society.

Whereas any intervention in the sacred rights of the individual is prohibited, the state on the other hand has always been good at granting protection and support for business. Roosevelt refers to this when he makes an important observation in his book, *Looking Forward*: "The same person who claims to want no interference in the life of business by the state and who means it most earnestly and with good reasons, is also the first person to run to Washington to demand a protective tax from Congress for his product. Then when circumstances deteriorate, which was the case in 1930, he will rush with the same speed back to the Congress of the United States to demand credit. The result is the Reconstruction Finance Corporation."

Basically that is the summary of the economic policies during the Presidency of Herbert Hoover. During his administration, when under the pressure of insurmountable human needs, first one and then another of the forty-eight States stepped forward to pass progressive unemployment insurance, and when, here and there, a progressive company took out unemployment insurance for its employees and white collar workers, the president still added his signature to a flyer issued by the National Manufacturers Association, also known as the Association of American Employers. This organization repeatedly spoke up against the "vicious and immoral alms system" of unemployment insurance. Hoover threw his entire weight on that side of the scale in order to save the principle, ironically labeled, "Help Yourself," and undeniably the principle that once had made America great. Shortly afterwards, however, Hoover established the Reconstruction Finance

Corporation as a credit agency, underwritten with billions of dollars, in order to redevelop destitute banks, railroad companies and industrial enterprises.

The latter became Hoover's final and only substantial attempt to bypass an economic downturn. The attempt fizzled, however, when this infusion into the money market remained ineffective and did not succeed in raising demand. It was foolish to pump credit into an idling industry that at best could only write off bankruptcy or use credit to further rationalize measures releasing them from new growth. As long as individual companies could improve their competitive edge with the credit from the Reconstruction Finance Corporation, the economy as a whole suffered and the stock market reacted symbolically to this attempt to stimulate the economy. A runaway speculative bull market was followed by an acute slump of new lows.

Of course the economic depression, by which Hoover's Presidency became identified, had far-reaching, earlier origins and could not simply be located in classic capitalism. It became not so much a functional crisis as a structural one. Without Roosevelt getting lost in theoretical discussions on the nature of the crisis, his remarks, previously made, pointed to the fact that he saw the crisis as structural and not functional. For him, the present is located in the slogan, "the uncertainty of market value," and the task of government, "the creation of economic statements and laws that support a regulated economy." Roosevelt sees in such endeavors as not just the right way to govern but also the one secure plumb line for a common economic structure. Roosevelt describes the danger lurking behind faith in automatic cycles as follows:

Many confess to the theory that a periodic slowdown in the economic engine is one of its basic functions, in other words, a function which we must cheerfully endure because if we try to circumvent it, we will only be ushering in a worse disaster. According to this theory, as far as I understand it, if we only smile long enough and keep our patience, in due time the economic engine will speed up again and after an uncertain amount of years, once more reach new peaks of what we shamefully have come to label prosperity. But that prosperity unfortunately is only the latest noticeable rotation of the economic engine before it succumbs to that secret underlying force of a slowdown again. To accept this underlying force, opposing our economic system, requires not only great stoicism but also strong faith in the unchangeable economic laws and to a lesser degree, faith in the competence of people being able to control what they have created even as I am able control my own body. Regardless of whether the theory contains definitive elements of truth, it asks human beings to put their hands in the pocket. I believe everyone suffers today because this convenient theory has implanted itself so firmly in the minds of some leaders both in the financial world and in government.

The deep structural crisis which broke out in the autumn of 1929, and which has now placed Roosevelt on an economic voyage of discovery, had its origins in the World War. One might even, as Roosevelt does, look for its genesis somewhere around the turn of the 20th century when the last frontier of the Union took on social formation and when the American continent lost its unique means of fighting the crisis. But with the War, America turned from being a debtor nation to being a creditor nation and by that turn she became one-thousand-fold drawn into the world's destitution. At the same time, unlimited possibilities for technical advances inherent in war production were discovered. America's young men at war served only eighteen months, yet that was time enough for the most powerful changes in the industrial production process to come about. (See appendix C.) The seeds of the American crisis lie in this technical revolution.

Suitable men, principally from the countryside, were recruited for military service and the call for labor-saving farm machinery grew especially loud. And so out of economic necessity, the tractor industry grew. Certainly there were tractors before the war. At the end of 1917, there were already 80,000 tractors in use on the American farm. But by the end of 1918, there were some 148,000 tractors. The industry credited its unheralded growth to the war, but also concluded that animal labor, too, could be replaced by tractors and that tractors were cheaper to use than human labor. The Texas Agricultural Experiment Station figured that for a cotton-picking farm of 200,000 acres, the cost of growing and harvesting with the use of a tractor was $668.00 vs. $1,524.00 by horsepower. Such exact accounting was probably not made everywhere. However, generally speaking, on certain large acreages costs could be reduced by half. In fact after the return of the army, victory parades with tractors continued to be part of the landscape. In the America of 1932, there are over one million tractors in operation on the American farm and with the same speed, American agriculture has freed itself from the use of harnessed animals. There were still twenty-six million horses and mules in use on the farm in 1918, but by 1928, that number had shrunk to nineteen million.

In addition to the tractor, the harvester-combine further revolutionized agriculture. This labor-saving machine mows, threshes and deposits the grain in a tank alongside the combine. The harvester-combine was already in operation across the wide, wheat-growing regions of the Northwest before the war, too. It would have taken a team of thirty-six horses to pull such a monster across the fields.

Now, it took only two men to operate the harvester-combine and one day's performance of a middle-sized machine would equal fifty to sixty mornings without. With the old binding machines, twenty mornings would equal a good day's work for two men on the harvester-combine. Therefore, the latter gradually eliminated the need for the migrant farm laborers who in the past were essential as they migrated west for the season. These seasonal workers came from the cities and industrial regions and moved from place to place with the harvest only to annoy the farmer's wives who saw them as seasonal nuisances. The harvester-combine now greatly reduced this form of migrant employment for the unemployed industrial laborer. However, the most important point was that the harvester-combine became profitable primarily on large acreages and therefore gave large farming enterprises an immediate advantage over smaller farms. For the average combine with a 4.80-meter cutting edge, the minimum limit of profitability was about 300 acres. The maximum use of the same machine could reach something like 1,000 acres. The Kansas Agricultural Experiment Station estimated that for 500 acres of wheat the cost of harvesting with an old binding and thrashing machine would be $4.41 per acre while with the harvester-combine it became $2.18 per acre. In other words, the cost was reduced by half.

Larger farms could credit their increased profitability to these facts. Secondly, at the same time the world price for wheat kept plunging to new lows. The combine added a temptation to expand cultivated land. Every substantial farmer tried to extend his area in order to realize the maximum profitability of the machine. But that extension contributed to the price of grain falling even further and the purchasing power of small and middle sized farms continued to plunge. In an effort to keep streamlining their production, smaller farmers took out mortgages that were liberally offered (the capital market was unusually liquid in those years) and the streamlining of agriculture celebrated ever new triumphs including the addition of new electric milking equipment for cows.

The glowing prosperity during these years already signaled the next phase of a capitalist economy. The drop in prices turned ever more threatening to agriculture and with the purchasing power of flat land collapsing under a merciless law, the hypothetical indebtedness of farmers rose to unjustifiable heights. Professor Studensky-Moskau researched the effects of the new agricultural technology in Volume 31 of the World Economic Archives and concluded, "The result will be the disappearance of the small, capitalized middle class and the saturation of the ranks of the working class." A study by Dr. Charles Galpin from the Department of Agriculture, confirmed the fact that during the years of the industrial boom, 1920 to 1927, the estimated number of indebted farmers reached over three million.

Even during the good years there was naturally always some unemployment in America. In addition to the exodus from the land between the years 1919 and 1927, the number of industrial jobs decreased from 11.5 to 10.7 million due to the streamlining of production. At the same time, the number of people employed in commerce rose from 4.5 to 6.1 million. The nature of every American phenomenon was this pace of change. This breakneck speed of change, which every European remembered as massive wastefulness with car dumps and other senseless disposals, became just as much a part of the American postwar prosperity as the world famous, high pressured American salesman. Long before the collapse in the fall of 1929, all the flow of business, and not only the stock market, had taken on speculative characteristics. That became the crux of the problem. When the war freed America, the great debtor nation, from its debts, America developed into the greatest land of promise on earth and the unsuspecting middle class lobbied for ever more industrial plants. There was a constant clamor in the air to invest.

The enormous continent was developed to its furthest boundaries. Factories shot up like mushrooms from the soil. Henry Ford estimated the life expectancy of a modern factory to be seven years at the most. Within seven years every industrial plant would become obsolete, in need of being torn down and replaced from the ground up with a new one. As fast as possible, new ground was breaking in the world of capitalism and the young country with its wealth was enjoying a happy honeymoon. A problem of over-production could not even be imagined during those years.

Intelligent and important Americans alike seriously believed to have found in the economy a perpetual upward momentum and a depression seemed once and for all to have been eliminated with a formula of higher wages, greater turnover and rising profits. The well-known American business leader Edward A. Filene, who still today has not learned to remain silent, at the time spoke these enthusiastic words, "The new entrepreneur has realized the socialist's dream even if not by socialist means. For the first time in the history of man, leisure and luxury will be portioned out to all and for the first time in humankind, a refinement of the people is in sight."

The secret of the golden era was to reside in an unending increase in the domestic market and in preventing a stoppage of the growing production. But in reality, an increase in wages was not able to keep in step with the growing production. According to the Bureau of Labor Statistics, the production per worker in the period between 1922 and 1927 rose by an annual average of 3.5 percent while their wages averaged only a 2.4 percent rise. Here is where the balance of the purchasing power in the industrial sector shifted.

When the danger of the domestic market becoming saturated first moved like a dark cloud over the country, a fatal optimism shifted focus instead to the foreign markets. Roosevelt graphically pictured this when he wrote:

> *As seen from the outside, it has been pointed out that the American public has been chosen to play the role of Alice in Wonderland. And let me add that Alice has seen these new economic theories in the mirror. The White Knight has babbled of unlimited potential foreign markets and prophesied ten years into the future. But the confused and slightly skeptical Alice has posed a few simple questions of her own:*

'Will the printing and selling of ever new stocks and

bonds, the building of new factories and the increase in performance not lead to the point where we make more goods than we can ever sell?'

'No, the more we produce the more we can sell,' the Chatter Box replies.

'And after we produce surpluses?'

'Oh, we will sell them to foreign consumers.'

'How can foreigners buy these surpluses?'

'We will lend them the money.'

'Ah, now I understand,' Alice responds. 'They will buy our surpluses with our own money... But how will the foreigners pay back these loans?'

'That's very simple. Haven't you heard yet of the deferment of payments plan?'

As childish as this may sound, here we have the essence of the magic formula of 1928.

This Munchhausen (18th-Century German Baron known for his tall tales) theory that one can pull oneself out of a swamp by holding on to a blade of grass, still found many believers. The theory seemed to work. Under the spell of this fable, the public offered their life savings on the altar of the Stock Market. Business people honestly convinced themselves that they had received expert advice and consequently put their solvency on volatile expansion. Bankers much too liberally issued credit not based on careful research and human reason fell silent before the magic of such economic sorcery.

The giddiness was followed by the collapse and the Depression came as predictably as Ash Wednesday follows the Carnival. Already in 1926, when a collapse was first on the horizon, the business community began to get queasy about the potential limits of individual markets and world trade hinted at a catastrophe in the making. However, it was still thought possible to avert a crisis by means of a substantial intervention, a magic trick which later essentially contributed to the chronic and almost unbeatable character of the crisis. This magic trick spelled an immediate repayment scheme to be organized in such a grandiose way as to maintain the beautiful weather called overproduction. Through such a repayment scheme, the salaries of regular wage earners would be mortgaged into the distant future in order to safeguard production orders. It meant skirting on the outer edges of the problem with eyes closed to the reality of continued overproduction. Everything about a decent American life, a reasonable American standard of living, was pushed onto the small consumer for repayment later – cars, vacuum cleaners, washing machines, brand new houses, fixtures and furniture, electric refrigerators and radios. Only when consumers with good conscience could no longer make even the smallest repayment did the magic trick unravel.

Had the crisis erupted already in 1926, perhaps a transition to a new economy might still have been worked out in a capitalist way. But because the economy would be held back from the warnings signs of 1927, 1928, and 1929 by dubious economic and psychological life supports, an enormous sheet of ice froze over demand that burdened even the smallest citizen. An enormous congestion of goods for years came to stuff the warehouses with a market-destroying amount of unpaid products that only after short use would reappear for sale in the trade at any price as second hand goods.

Hoover's time in office was shaped by the politics of the small middle class. Maybe like most of his fellow countrymen, Hoover had seen the collapse of Wall Street in October 1929 when like a brief summer shower before the sun breaks out again, stocks lost two-fifths or more of their value in the course of one day. But the lightning and thunderstorm that this time crisscrossed the entire globe became only the prelude for a prolonged soaking rain that would reach from Wall Street to every corner of the world.

Hoover's politics allowed for a short formula to be tried during these same years. Wall Street had lost a gamble; keeping the peace remained the civic duty of the president. In the autumn, Hoover hoped for an economic rebound in the economy by spring and in the spring, he did something to give the Stock Market a short boost. The following autumn, everything was postponed again until spring. An official estimate of the number of unemployed was released, regularly registering one to two million lower than most reliable private estimates. Regardless, a number of twelve million was finally agreed upon. Hoover convened a special conference of experts to address the problem of unemployment in the fall of 1930. They met behind closed doors for long hours and many days and were completely ignored by the public. A business journalist once commented, "The conference concluded that unemployment would end as soon as the unemployed went back to work."

To fight the crisis, Hoover also mobilized public resources and released billions of additional credit through the Reconstruction Finance Corporation. This money, however, did not provide funding for public works. It was to support more private initiatives. The private sector did not use the stimulation money as long as the warehouses were still full and opportunities for sales were not visible on the horizon. Therefore, the credit from the Reconstruction Finance Corporation had no real effect for it did not serve the function of credit; instead of serving as credit in the true sense of the word, it became a subsidy poured into a bottomless barrel.

FOUR
Forerunner to the Revolution

THE LAST MONTHS before the new transition in the White House became a time of merciless criticism. The change in administration was portrayed as a revolutionary event. And revolutions never appear without good reason. To the historic forerunner of the Roosevelt revolution belong all the critical comments of the last six months starting March 4, 1932. While the criticisms supplied Roosevelt with weapons during his campaign, they now provided a huge emotional backdrop for the revolution about to be carried forth.

Of all the critical comments, the report by the Committee on Social Development for America is taken most seriously. President Hoover first called the committee, composed of scientists with impressive names, in 1929 and at the time, entrusted it with the task to present an extensive study of the current social developments and to provide insight into the future. The scientific research of the committee cost several million dollars and presents the most comprehensive study of the social situation in the United States to date.

When Hoover assembled the committee, American faith in an economic machine with perpetual forward momentum was still in full bloom. It might therefore be expected for such a report on enlightened American capitalism to be heralded as one sanctioned by science. But something else occurred. The official report appeared at the end of December, 1932. In the report, based on scientific research, the commission speaks quite openly about the danger signs of a looming revolution. It implies a revolution from the ground up.

If stronger agreement about job performance coupled with social objectives cannot be achieved beyond what is apparently done today to train the young, it is not at all certain that we will be able to avoid an overwhelming revolution. The committee does not want to adopt the posture of alarmed irresponsibility but, on the other hand, were we to handle the facts carelessly and gloss over the rough and bitter realities in the business sector we would be lying about the threatening dangers even as our heavy industrial equipment moves over crumbling streets and swaying bridges. There are times when silence is no longer neutrality but rather a nod of consent.

Upon the issue of the report, Hoover added a short but grim preface. "It was the task of the committee to present investigations into changes available for implementation; instead the findings accentuate the former elements in our social structure upon which our stability rested before instability set in."

In the difficult shake-up of the status quo, the report points to the dubious increase of production during the past decade. Almost daily, one reporter speaks of the astonishing contrast between the wonderful technical achievement of some unbelievable skyscraper and the enormous backwardness of an equally unbelievable slum. Another expresses it no less graphically, "A nation does not advance by dynamic energy alone but also by keeping in balance her various strengths...an unequal rate of growth...leads to danger zones and points of tension. It is the same principle as when the various organs of the physical body or the individual parts of an automobile fail to work together in harmony."

The capitalist society, according to the committee, is mainly composed of self-serving individuals, groups and classes confronted with the ideal of a society where everyone should strive for the wellbeing of the whole. The report warns against impulsive reactions to this statement but also avoids setting new ground rules.

The committee only recommends that social steps be pushed to keep in line with technical progress. Such a recommendation resonates with a remark already attributed to Roosevelt's Brain Trust and the following excerpt from the report resembles Roosevelt's own philosophy even more strongly.

The goal of all known authority over the destinies of a people is to create greater harmony between what has been endowed by nature and what civilization is able to provide. Social insight and the extensive application of new knowledge become the means of achieving this harmony. It will remain the responsibility of the collective wisdom of many minds for years to come. Both insight and invention are social achievements forged from countless individual experiences. The categories named will be exhausted by nothing less than the combined intelligence of the nation. Concurrently, the committee cannot overestimate the role of reasoning in social life. Every social action surely is the result over time of the application of modern science and educated intelligence to every effort.

Present circumstances come under sharp criticism and the facts can hardly be denied. Reporters repeatedly call for a serious analysis of the available options for development, be it more planning or less drifting with the tide. The American federal system of individual states always applied reasonable brakes to business cycles in the past but the system is now confronted with this absolutely crushing report.

The economic problems of the New World have increasingly come to resemble the problems of the old world. Within a decade, American capitalism due to a complete lack of planning and setting boundaries has proceeded to the point of absurdity. Logically, the years of prosperity might only continue if the whole world opens itself to the United States and gives America a single, gigantic market. The detailed report emphasizes certain main points from which all new prospective planning should proceed. It is worthwhile going into more detail here since Roosevelt's own economic policies are based on many of the same main points.

According to the report, the United States registered a decline in population in the last decade and based on other statistics, it can be assumed the total population of America might reach a maximum of 146 million between 1960 and 1970. Combined with a decline in natural growth, at the same time the number of older people in the population can be expected to increase. If the ages between twenty and sixty-four are considered the years of productive employment, then the unit number of producer per consumer was 1.67 in 1930. The projected number, however, for 1950 will be 1.59. The capitalist economy for expansion basically rests on the natural growth of the population. As natural growth slows, problems arise. All arms of production will have to deal with less flexible consumption per head, as for example in agriculture when production capability recently exceeded the former demand. At various times when birth rates in the population drop the result is neither a more desirable population number nor a population of the highest quality. Should employment opportunities in the United States fail to return, there is always the danger of an exploding farm population of millions settling on virgin land, adding stress to agriculture while creating a self-sustaining farm economy with a much lower living standard.

In many cases, this has proved disastrous for agriculture when no fertilizer gets applied to the land. Furthermore, land erosion is big problem, too, and if not stopped, a quarter of the arable surface currently under cultivation could become useless for farming within fifty years. Farm production between 1922 and 1926 rose twenty-seven percent despite the decline in farm labor. There are still great opportunities available to increase farm production per unit of labor but the current problem is a contracting farm economy. As with the expansion, this problem cannot be left to the initiative of individual farmers alone. Roosevelt is taking the first practical steps here.

America's natural resources are great but not inexhaustible. From 1899 to 1929 the population grew by 62 percent, the mining of minerals by 286 percent, the new supply of labor-saving machinery, discounting automobiles, by 536 percent, and inclusive of automobiles by 2,510 percent. These figures point to the enormous increase in the productivity of labor. In mining there is constant back and forth between improved mining techniques and price increases due to the extraction of the most easily available deposits. In American mining today there are also signs of the first period of unplanned exploitation being over so that the costs of mining are rising as has been the situation in Europe for some time. And yet, the whole mining industry currently suffers from over expansion and over production. This leads to the depletion of indispensable mineral resources. Every year, 150 million tons of mineable coal remains in the ground under circumstances which make later extraction most unlikely. Similar waste is driving oil. The roots of the problem lie in the established statutes for the ownership of mineral resources, inherited from the Tudors in England. "It becomes necessary to control devaluation caused by unholy competition." (A thought also frequently quoted by Roosevelt).

Likewise, uncontrolled exploitation will affect the enormous forest resources of the United States. For the past twelve years, the yearly consumption of lumber amounted to roughly four times the yearly quota for new growth while the profit margin in all likelihood shrunk. Again, this problem cannot to be left to the purchasing power of the individual because the depressed price for wood makes it unprofitable for the private entrepreneur to care about reforestation. (Roosevelt's special interest and dedication to national reforestation is well known, too.)

Between 1922 and 1929, the levels of production in agriculture, mining and industry in relationship to the population grew twice as fast as before the War. Such increases, however, benefited production in far greater measure than it benefited the consumer. In the category of consumer products, durable goods such as houses and automobiles prevailed while, like the population, the manufacture of food, textiles and shoes slowed. The consumer in a capitalist economy holds an autonomous position. He has contributed greatly to the deepening crisis in America because he has allowed himself for years to be persuaded to buy on credit. The society is satisfied with keeping the purchasing power of the individual, like one's healthcare in middle age, an area of private anarchy. During the Depression, symptoms have recurred suggesting a return to a more primitive means of survival. Add to this a widespread return to a cashless exchange which enabled about one million Americans to subsist last winter. Similar to the case of Germans during the War, the sale of shoe leather for "self help" shoe repair in Ten Cent stores soared and the phenomena of "self help" across the country even created a new situation of people constructing their own coffins.

Over-expansion has also made itself felt in public transportation, road construction and the development of outlying towns for prospective settlement. In the areas around New York there is currently more than enough vacant land available to easily accommodate the many who are expected to flock to New York between today and 1960. In Detroit between 1920 and 1927, enough land was parceled out quickly in order to accommodate a sevenfold increase in population.

Finally concerning politics, the report states that the influence of political parties depends increasingly on the role of large interest groups. There are seven large corporations in the United States each employing more workers and earning more profit than any of the 48 individual states with the exception of New York. Such facts must inevitably lead to more serious considerations in new government regulations being given to the larger organized groups of society. In the most recent past, little has changed in the position of government. It maintains "indifference or even hostility towards various social proposals in a world of private property, democracy and parliamentary government of questionable acts." Roosevelt responds to the report as follows: "We can predict with certainty that in the future it will be impossible to evade serious and frank discussions on the meaning of democracy and capitalism. A much more forceful constructive or destructive change will become unavoidable as has become apparent during these past years. A weak government will be disastrous whether it refrains from social reform or attempts it."

The report of the Committee offers no sweeping programs for reform. It touches only on a few points some of which reappear in Roosevelt's legislative agenda. Among other things, the report suggests that a progressive taxation still be more rigorous for higher income brackets and that limits be established for inherited wealth. It allows for the expansion of public ownership and entertains the possibility of enlarging the list of public utilities to include industries, especially coal, insurance companies already being subject to such legislation.

Only a few important points relating to the current American situation can be lifted from the extensive 1,500-page report. Nevertheless, the Hoover Committee's report makes a strong impression on Congress and national leaders earnestly concerned about current U. S. planning and the country as a whole. Such concern considerably eases the introduction of Roosevelt's economic plans. At the same time, criticisms of the prevailing economic and social conditions were only silenced after Roosevelt took his first energetic steps towards radical reform. The welfare apprenticeship that in some way prepares for the Roosevelt Revolution is known as technocracy. Technocracy originated with a few professors at New York's Columbia University who merge a critique of the capitalist economic system with their own design for a crisis-free economy based on completely different preconditions. Technocracy brings the bankruptcy of the capitalist system to the attention of the general public in a country where the foundations for a functioning capitalism, liquid money, capital markets, and the absence of foreign debt, already exist.

The historic significance of the technocrats is their propaganda. America historically was the laboratory of capitalism where laws could freely evolve and where one, like in a test tube, could observe the functions and failures of capitalism. Now, from the technocrats' test tube, capitalism looks as follows:

1. Technical advances have made possible in wonderful ways increased production with a smaller workforce. There are countless examples of this. It took seventy hours of labor in 1900 to produce a ton of steel and only thirteen hours in 1929. It took three hundred and thirteen man hours to produce an automobile in 1919 and only ninety-two hours in 1929. These facts are commonly understood, nowhere denied and countless similar examples recorded.

2. The speed of technological advance leads to unemployment. This insight dates back already to Karl Marx and can also be substantiated with many examples. Progressive cigarette manufacturers claim that no human hand has touched their cigarettes until a cigarette is found in the smoker's hand. Today, there are 2,000 to 3,000 cigarettes being produced per minute per worker per diem while a few years ago it was only possible to make 500 to 600 cigarettes per minute. The latest advances in prefabricated houses allow for the separate parts of a house to be delivered, finished and assembled at their final destination. This development has led to desperate resistance movements on the part of other manufacturers. It is today also technically possible to produce an absolutely indestructible razorblade that might last a lifetime even on the toughest beard. It would cost approximately thirty cents to make but because of opposition from the manufacturers, such a new razorblade is still not being commercially produced.

3. Technical advances lead to the decline of the economic

system of capitalism. This lesson, too, has at least one forerunner in Karl Marx. Products today will not be produced for use as much as for profit. All profit extracted in currency will immediately be translated into some kind of credit. Even the bank notes we hold in our hands are nothing more than a debenture bond of the issuing bank. Rapid technological progress leads inevitably to increasingly rapid indebtedness. Many technical plants become obsolete and are sacrificed to new streamlining before their original purchasing price is even amortized. And because every streamlining measure requires new loans, debt piles upon debt.

For years in America, indebtedness has already grown faster than production and production faster than the population. For example, one of the large American railroad companies borrowed about three hundred and ten million dollars to build its rail lines and according to the requirements of the loan, three million dollars of this sum will be due by 1948. Another million will fall due in 1969 and by 1997 one hundred and six million dollars must be paid back in one lump payment. The rest of the debt of approximately two hundred million must be procured by the year, 2047, in order to pay for our present day convenience and comfort.

Incredible progress in all areas is driven forward by the momentum of reinvestments. People enjoying the yields of the capitalist economy cannot possibly use all their income on consumption. Therefore, the only other possibility becomes to reinvest to create value. For example, Henry Ford, his wife, and son are the sole owners of 172,654 shares of Ford Company stock. In 1930, each shared earns a dividend of $257.00. What can three individuals possible do with a yearly income of forty-four million dollars even if they consider buying all of the world's antique furniture? The drive to reinvest has pushed the rationalization for investment to the point where today the interest rates in America approach zero. Recently in New York, a working loan of three months yielded only half a percent in interest.

According to the technocrats, the capitalist system is moving towards its own destruction for the following reasons: higher wages and with them, increased purchasing power of consumers, in the capitalist system dependent on working hours. Meanwhile, technological advances continue to shrink the hours necessary for work. Instead of sharing the time among many laborers it takes to make a product, the capitalist system forces the employer to free himself as much as possible from human labor, substituting the better alternative of machine labor. Whether intentionally or not, the capitalist system destroys consumers and with them its own life support, the market.

The technocrats prophesy that if current trends continue America will have twenty million unemployed in two years and that the prevailing Depression will lead to the collapse of the capitalist economic system. They see the solution in bringing the natural resources of the country into harmonious balance with the consumers. According to the technocrats, the United States is the next country in the world to become self sufficient. It has fifty percent of the world's coal deposits, forty percent of the iron ore, sixty-nine percent of the oil deposits and eighty-five percent of all sources of natural gas. Just over six percent of the world's population resides in an area that is just one twelfth of the world's landmass and that contains perhaps half of all the world's energy deposits. In such circumstances there is no reason for poverty in the United States. With the planned development of the country's natural resources and with a division of labor among all able-bodied, everyone should be able to reach a higher standard of living with lower work quotas. In this way, the human being will stop being a slave to technology and instead bring technology to humankind's service. Money that fluctuates in value shall be eliminated and replaced with an energy certificate, based on a certain amount of energy and such energy certificates shall be voided as soon as they have fulfilled their function in purchasing a product.

The essential features of this theory came to dominate public discourse in America for several months prior to Roosevelt taking the oars of state. The discourse includes a deep skepticism of traditional views, a position that often acts as the prelude to an effective revolution. The theory and its anti-capitalist tenor seems revolutionary and was quickly maligned, albeit unfairly, with the label, "Made in Soviet Russia." Such a label immediately serves as a frightening warning and from this time on, capable immigration officials began to question applicants for immigration if they hold revolutionary ideas and a new blank space on the application form appears for the question of whether the applicant believes in technology or not.

The technological theory stirs the emotions of the public for only a short time. But many of the fundamental ideas of the technocrats nevertheless continue in the Roosevelt administration, including the reflections on a stable domestic currency, economic functions of the purchasing power, systematic planning and policies of national self sufficiency. These ideas float in the air, so to speak, and the Roosevelt revolution does not emerge unexpectedly. For the most part, the economic crisis has prepared the way for Roosevelt. The complete failure of the government and economic leaders of the opposition to tackle the ever growing problems of the collapse of private charities and the exhaustion of public funds makes room for Roosevelt's leadership and strong resolve. Hoover's Committee for the Investigation of Social Developments upheld in its report the example of how America faced changes caused by the World War, changes which proved what a people is capable of when push comes to shove. During the war, the entire nation's economic life was placed under direct government control and the energies of a whole continent concentrated on a clearly defined goal. According to the report the mobilization fulfilled its purpose despite the waste and confusion which the sudden change in the orientation towards war brought about. It is a clear illustration of the speed with which people in an emergency can change their basic orientation. However, will the same human capacity to promote public welfare be taken as seriously as our generation pursued total victory in war?

But in the end, President Hoover paved the way for the Roosevelt revolution not only by what he omitted but also by what he tried to do. During the course of the Depression, Hoover more often than not favored higher wages and the stretching of work through the maintenance of a larger workforce. Hoover's appeals have only modest results but they unintentionally at least acknowledge the principle that in the national economy the common interest must rank higher than pure profitability; the individual cannot just do or refrain from doing what he wants to do or not.

Throughout the Depression, Hoover more or less frequently admitted to the principle that it is a duty of the community to care for the innocent victims of a breakdown even at the same time as Hoover hesitated to remove from the hands of private charity the distribution of unemployment welfare. As far as social obligations are understood, the next step is basically to avoid economic collapses from the beginning by controlling the money supply, capital markets and production.

Hoover took a further step in this direction when he established the Reconstruction Finance Corporation. 1.2 billion dollars in public funds were to be distributed to support troubled banks and railroad companies, and still larger sums reserved if more money were needed. Such an "initial ignition" of credit was expected to lift the economy but the economy still failed to ignite. For America an extraordinarily important new precedent, however, was set in motion. In a crisis, the state will sacrifice itself. It will save from insolvency large private enterprises and therefore rescue them from the capitalist downturns of economic events.

No gun salute filled the air on March 4, 1933, when Franklin Delano Roosevelt took over the leadership of the most powerful nation in the world. The country almost immediately stalled again with bank failures. Nothing symbolizes the end of a historic period more than the collapse of the world's most powerful banking system. President Hoover was close to a nervous breakdown; a few days later, he fell into a deep depression in a New York hotel. But on the white marble steps of the Capitol in Washington a strong, dynamic-looking man stood tall despite being supported by two crutches. The ceremony was bathed in the bright luminescence of March sunshine. The man who now assumed responsibility for the country heard the cheering crowds and at the same time, the American people welcomed his clear, calm voice over the radio.

The practices of unscrupulous money changers stand indicted in the court of public opinion and rejected in the hearts and minds of men. It is true they have tried, but their efforts have been cast in the pattern of an outworn tradition. Faced with the failure of credit they have proposed only the lending of more money. Stripped of the lure of profit, by which to induce our people to follow their false leadership, they have resorted to exhortations and tearfully pleaded for restored confidence. They know only the rules of a generation of self-seekers. They have no vision, and where there is no vision the people perish.

The money changers have fled from their high seats in the temple of our civilization. Now, may we restore that temple to the ancient truths. The means of the restoration lies in the extent to which we apply social values that are nobler than mere monetary profit.

If I read the temper of our people correctly, we now realize as we have never realized before our interdependence on each other. We cannot merely take but we must give as well. If we are to go forward, we must move as a trained and loyal army willing to sacrifice for the common good with discipline because without such discipline, no progress can be made and no leadership become effective. I know we are ready and willing to submit our lives and property to such discipline because discipline makes possible a leadership which aims at a larger good. This I propose to offer, pledging that larger purposes will bind upon us, yes, bind upon us all, like a sacred obligation, a unity of duty hitherto evoked only in time of armed strife.

With this pledge taken, I unhesitatingly assume the leadership of this great army of our people dedicated to a disciplined attack upon our common problems. But in the event that the Congress shall fail to take one of these two courses and in the event that the national emergency is still critical, I shall not evade the clear course of duty that will then confront me. I shall ask the Congress for the one remaining instrument to meet the crisis – broad Executive Power to wage war against the emergency, a power as great as the one that would be given me if in fact we were invaded by a foreign foe.

The people of the United States have not failed. In their need, they have registered a mandate. They want direct, vigorous action. They have asked for discipline and direction through leadership. They have made me the present instrument of their wishes. In the spirit of their gift, I receive it.

Dr. Schachts and Dr. Luthers with the president.

Hoover and Roosevelt on route to the inauguration.

FIVE

The Mood to Experiment

_____

CLEAR SEPARATIONS OR distinctions between proposed legislative programs and the governmental actions that follow are generally expected of any new administration, for once legislative programs come up against the harsh realities of governing the tasks at hand are almost always more complicated than the proposed agendas. Count Mirabeau, the 18th-century French politician, at one time expressed it this way, "A Jacobean minister is not necessarily a Jacobean minister." Roosevelt challenges this distinction however, for he knows that the public expects strict adherence to his proposed legislative programs and immediately upon taking office, Roosevelt issued a book with the latest statistics already gathered during his first days in office. This book, fresh with Roosevelt's impetuosity, is entitled, *Looking Forward.*

In this book, Roosevelt compiles anew the most important speeches and articles issued during the time of his presidential campaign. He clearly outlines all that he promised the American people while on the campaign trail. The book, however, is more than a collection of campaign speeches. It is a declaration of Roosevelt's revolutionary beliefs and yet, Roosevelt is not a revolutionary of holy wrath. He is a revolutionary with a sober awareness of the situation. His life and aristocratic heritage forbid him to take on revolutionary extremes. He approaches the revolution with fresh insight into how our economic and political lives are interconnected. Roosevelt is, so to speak, *a revolutionary with common sense.* Nothing escapes his empathic heart.

Roosevelt definitely does not perceive himself to be a

revolutionary. Early in life, he considered himself a conservative in the European sense of the word. Conservative in the American vocabulary equates more with the German understanding of reactionary but a reactionary Roosevelt absolutely is not. Roosevelt's former conservative spirit finds expression again and again, whether in reference to American history, especially Jefferson, or in statements such as, "faith in America, faith in our traditions of personal responsibility, faith in our institutions, and faith in ourselves cause us to look for new interpretations of the old social contracts." The country shall "stand once more on the principles on which it was founded." Such an inner connection between Roosevelt's revolutionary ideas and deeper conservative understanding of government seem to skeptics as fake and foreign and at odds with his proposed agenda. In this respect, however, Roosevelt perhaps most strongly resembles the great former German statesman, Baron von Stein, 1757-1831.

In summary, what stands out most strongly are Roosevelt's courage and determination to experiment.

> *The country needs it, and if I really understand the mood of the country, it is supportive of persistent and bold experimentation. The healthy human mind encourages us to adopt and try a plan; if it fails, give it up and try something else. But above all, try something. The millions who suffer want will not stand silently by forever while the means to satisfy their daily needs are within easy reach. We need powerful ideas, enthusiasm and the determination bravely to face the facts head on even if they are unpleasant. When it is an emergency, more drastic measures are called for to correct the errors that currently cause the suffering in our economic system. We need the courage of youth.*

The resolute will for reform earned Roosevelt the reputation of revolutionary already during his campaign while Hoover remained the man who would save us from such experimentation. In the eyes of Roosevelt's opponents, Roosevelt is a socialist; attempts to vilify him with this label, however, thoroughly fail.

What then might Roosevelt's socialism actually look like in practice? Roosevelt proceeds from the premise that "our economic life is in the hands of some six hundred enterprises that control two thirds of American industry. Ten million small entrepreneurs are left to divide the remaining third. It is often said that we are heading straight towards an economic oligarchy if we have not reached it already." According to Roosevelt, the disproportionate distribution of wealth is not representative of the American ideal and is the result of years of unplanned development. Roosevelt therefore supports a change in basic values. Roosevelt wants to remove the problem of under-consumption, change the uneven distribution of available products and place the current economic system in the service of the people. The question of purchasing power remains at the center of his discussions. Based on Roosevelt's prediction, "we stand on the threshold of fundamental change in our economic thinking." In the future, more thought will be given to consumers and less to producers. "We will not be able to straighten our sick economic system if we do not deliver a wiser and fairer distribution of our national income at the same time."

According to Roosevelt, the inventive human spirit that first created this great social and economic machine has the ability to nurture it so that, at least, it may be able to provide every willing and able worker with the necessary requirements for living. In such a system the average daily wage must become more substantial than before and the capital gains, especially from speculation, become less.

With his emphasis on the economic importance of purchasing power, Roosevelt takes enlightened American capitalism at its word. The American form of post-war capitalism, which theoretically liked to be called welfare capitalism, new entrepreneurship, or even the business of economics, recognizes the importance of higher wages. Henry Ford states the same in a succinct way when he says, "The six dollar wage per shift is more economical than the five dollar wage." However, he admits that when he adds a dollar, the production belt also has to move a little faster in order for the same dollar to be regained. Therefore Henry Ford tersely adds, "But how far it might go, I do not know." Could it not be assumed that Roosevelt's strong emphasis on higher wages would be applauded in the area of enlightened capitalism? It is exactly from this point of view that the formula for rising wages, growing turnover and bigger profits is promoted as sound business principle. But in reality, statistics show that profits rise faster than wages and turnover. Therefore, Roosevelt reframes the formula to read "rising wages, growing turnover, smaller profits." During the presidential campaign, Roosevelt therefore received scant support from the side of enlightened capitalism. Hoover was seen as the safer candidate. And Henry Ford simply lowers his famous six dollar wage to four dollars per shift.

Roosevelt's book, *Looking Forward*, enumerates the essential ideas that resurface in the first months of his administration, ideas that now take the form of draft legislation. He speaks about the increase of the price of goods within a reasonable economic climate and preaches the value of an honest dollar whereby today's purchasing power can be maintained a generation later. He wants to help reduce agricultural surpluses for the farmer and to substitute former commercial practices with foreign treaties. Roosevelt plans to reorganize, streamline and make all government departments more frugal and efficient, especially local governing bodies that still belong to the time of the oxcarts. He favors the abandonment of farmland that no longer is economical for farming and insists on planned reforestation. He envisions decentralizing industry and relocating these same industries partly in the countryside. Roosevelt hopes in this way to create a new subgroup of the population which is neither made up of farmers or laborers exclusively but known as a "land-industrial" class. An extensive road building project will become important to attain this goal.

Furthermore, Roosevelt speaks to the issues of crime and justice reform. But above everything else, Roosevelt's concern is for the forgotten man, the two categories of people who have suffered the most under the present circumstances, i.e. farmers and laborers. Given this concern, Roosevelt's push for huge projects and for stability in market forces becomes understandable. Extensive public works must help overcome an economic depression in times of crisis and stability in employment must be attempted through planned cooperation and the elimination of murderous competition. Another avenue for the advancement of stability in employment is the introduction of unemployment insurance with costs to be carried by employers. And in order to protect the consumer from exploitation, Roosevelt wants to place relief agencies in public hands. Finally, he hopes at the same time to lift both rural and land-industrial living standards. A considerable component of the agenda is the demand for natural water resources for all times to remain in the public's possession. This idea is as radical as the American principle of freedom and the formation of the United States itself. "As long as I am president, the government shall never relinquish its sovereignty nor right to control the energy reserves of this country."

In face of a crisis-mounting speculation, Roosevelt wants to provide a thorough and comprehensive explanation for the failure of capital management. He presents his own constructive thoughts. His comments on the failure of business leaders and their sacrosanct principles are often nasty and his critique of the unscrupulous deception of the public by the stock exchange, bitter and harsh. Roosevelt floats the creation of a genuine harmony of interests as the ideal, an ideal probably best described in Germany as the economic side of community. When Ramsay MacDonald arrived in Washington, he brought along Roosevelt's book, which had just been published, and when he finished reading it, MacDonald is supposed to have shaken his head and exclaimed, "Just like Hitler."

Roosevelt's book is indirectly co-written by The Brain Trust for it is the Brain Trust and especially Professor Raymond Moley who assisted Roosevelt with the campaign speeches now included in the book. Even though the book shows Roosevelt's overall temperament in powerful visual images, it also shows the outpouring of an intelligent and charismatic orator as he stands on the spiritual foundations of new economic thought. Roosevelt's future vision of the state and the economy first originates in the minds of the Brain Trust and the vision now accompanies Roosevelt to the White House.

There are three groups of advisors in Roosevelt's inner circle. The first and most tightly knit of these three groups is the so-called Bettrand-Cabinet, named after Bettrand de la Borderie (1594-1632). It is composed of Mrs. Roosevelt, Louis McHenry Howe, Roosevelt's old friend and secretary, and Professor Raymond Moley and it forms the nucleus of the Brain Trust. The Bettrand-Cabinet originated during the years when Roosevelt was paralyzed and bedridden at which time he clarified and deepened his world view through conversations about Bettrand and by voluminous reading. Ever since that time, the Bettrand-Cabinet maintains the task and authority to finalize the plans for each day with the president by breakfast-time which Roosevelt usually takes in bed. According to American public opinion, the Bettrand-Cabinet connotes something strange and mysterious. Resolutions are often decided upon in these unofficial Bettrand-Cabinet meetings, resolutions which do not again resurface during the day and are often dropped from other conferences.

Equally shrouded in myth but somewhat larger than the Bettrand-Cabinet, is the group called the Brain Trust. It is composed of professors and men from practical walks of life who have been Roosevelt's advisors from the time when he was governor of New York. It is often suggested that Brain Trust does not imply a gathering of the most celebrated minds of the nation. The majority of its members, before they entered the limelight of

Washington with Roosevelt, are hardly known outside the academic circles of their universities and their narrow academic specialties. It is important to note that those professors with the most impressive names, Charles Tuassig, Charles E. Merriam, William Ogburn and Harold Moulton, do not carry the highest rank within the Brain Trust.

The Brain Trust is quite different from President Coolidge's advisory circle of enlightened intellects, remembered as the "best minds" who could never reach an agreement precisely because of their enlightenment. The Brain Trust includes young professors in no need of being top authorities but for whom a balance of intellectual principles is important. Furthermore, they act more as Roosevelt's assistants than as his advisors. Roosevelt alone is the honored leader and head of the circle and it is his directives for a new era that are primarily addressed. The same holds true for the third and largest circle, Roosevelt's cabinet made up of the heads of the individual government departments. Roosevelt here, too, does not choose to surround himself with the most prominent members of the Democratic Party although that would have been easy. He appoints more second-tier leaders and individuals who nevertheless comprise a first-rate cabinet. This is especially true of the three ministers responsible for stimulating the economy through the National Reconstruction Administration: Henry Wallace, minister of agriculture, Harold Ickes, minister of the interior, and Daniel Roper, minister of commerce.

The minister of agriculture, Henry Wallace, was quite unknown before his call to Roosevelt's cabinet. People in his home state of Iowa know him only as editor of the *Iowa Farmer* and his father, a leading Republican, is much better known than his son. But his talents grow with the new responsibilities given him in the Roosevelt cabinet and he shows himself to be the right person with endless patience in persuading farmers to accept a reduction in the cultivation of their land.

The minister of the interior, Harold Ickes, originally also

comes from the Republican Party albeit the progressive camp of the Republicans. Before his appointment to the cabinet, he had a reputation of being a highly qualified and respected Chicago lawyer who was by no means popular as a politician. Today in the cabinet, he holds the key management responsibilities for mining, petroleum and forestry and as the minister of oil management, Ickes has an extremely influential voice. In his hands rest the most difficult government negotiations with the oil industry.

Finally, the minister of commerce, Daniel Roper, also heralds from the practice of law. At the party convention in Chicago in 1932, he played a decisive role when he showed the friends of Roosevelt how to break the power of Al Smith and John Raskob, Chairman of the National Democratic Committee. Within the Democratic Party, their group represents the old principles of capitalism. Roper is the minister of railroads today in addition to being the one responsible for the reorganization of relief agencies.

Without doubt, the most important of the three inner circles is the Intelligence or better known Brain Trust, also nicknamed "the Great Soviet Thinkers" in popular American parlance. Roosevelt likewise plays on words when he quips that it should be called "Trust Brains," as in abandoning oneself to brains. The Brain Trust becomes the all-encompassing name and the Brain Trust emphasizes fact finding, as in relying on facts based on academic knowledge.

From the beginning, the Brain Trust evolved from the Bettrand-Cabinet when Roosevelt was first confined with polio. Mrs. Roosevelt and Mr. Howe count as its oldest members. Throughout the years, Mrs. Roosevelt repeatedly linked her husband's interests with the social concerns she nurtures through her many interactions with schools, women's and children's welfare agencies. She continues to participate in many of these agencies today and according to her public following, ties the various tasks which fall on the First Lady of the land together in rare harmony with her many obligations and social work interests.

Mr. Howe's character and personal influence on the president are frequently disputed. Roosevelt and Howe first crossed paths as early as 1910 when Howe was an insignificant reporter in Albany. When he came to know the young state senator, Howe was supposed to have spoken this prophetic word referring to Roosevelt, "He is carved from presidential wood." Ever since, Howe dedicated his life to Roosevelt's future. He followed Roosevelt to the ministry of the navy in Washington, traveled with the Roosevelt family wherever it went, be it Albany, New York or Hyde Park, and when Roosevelt became afflicted with debilitating polio, stayed with him to make sure Roosevelt would recover in time. After twenty-two years as Roosevelt's friend and twenty as his special crony, Howe is probably the President's most intimate confidant. It is no wonder that the influence of this man of small statue with gnome-like features, unable to climb ten steps without having to catch his breath, becomes absolutely legendary.

This much is certain, however. Howe's devotion is to a person rather than to an ideology. His thoughts are exclusively focused on the career of one man, Franklin Delano Roosevelt. In terms of energy and readiness to sacrifice in the service of his job, Howe does not stand far behind Roosevelt's own devotion. Perhaps Howe is only a little less electable than Roosevelt with the electorate of the middle. Whenever Roosevelt suddenly scores a big punch, the idea first originates with Howe.

Howe remains tireless in the service of Roosevelt. For years, he managed Roosevelt's extensive correspondence with hundreds and thousands of citizens throughout the country. No farmer, no matter how remote the region of his farm, is ever too insignificant or unworthy for a long, four-page letter from Roosevelt and such correspondence results in the overwhelming conviction that Roosevelt cares about the unique concerns of each farmer. Howe embodies the role of friend, accomplice, advisor, manager and fact finder all in one. He completes political tasks as carefully as household chores. Even if Mrs. Roosevelt is in need of advice, she turns to Howe and whenever a member of the family travels, it is

Howe who obtains the tickets and makes sure the suitcases arrive at the station in time. He is a hundred percent content to stand next to his boss and to blot the signature Roosevelt applies to his letters. And Howe completes the most difficult political tasks with the same precision. After a full day of work, Howe returns to his room, lies down on his bed and enjoys detective stories. In sum, he demands nothing of himself other than to serve his friend.

Howe is short of stature, reserved by nature and quite unpopular in crowds. Many repeatedly complain about his unfriendly personality. Such complaints were voiced again recently but Roosevelt just laughs and contributes them to Howe's egocentricity. Roosevelt appreciates what a committed friend Howe is. Compared to Woodrow Wilson's Colonel Edward M. House, these two men share only the same shortness of statute and similar sounding names.

Professor Raymond Moley is considered the most important personality and top brain in the Brain Trust. His friendship with Roosevelt also dates back many years. Roosevelt calls Moley, "Ray" and Moley addresses the president as "Governor." Raymond Moley began his career as a criminologist and Roosevelt first became aware of Moley's written work on the criminal underworld at a time when Roosevelt also focused attention on this problem in New York State and as a result, made good progress in fighting crime and granting probations in New York. Roosevelt now hopes to make these same lessons applicable to the entire country. More important to Roosevelt than Moley's theories on criminal justice and practice, however, are his opinions on the best form of government.

Ray Moley entertains considerable doubt about the functioning of democracy. He admits to having lost belief in numbers as a means of reaching the most desirable political solutions. Instead of confidence in the wisdom of a few votes, he claims to have faith in facts. "I am not so sure," Moley succinctly says, "that the current situation supports our trust in the suitability of parliamentary government, at least not as we see it at the present time. We live in a world that is different from the former when democratic principles were first designed." Moley is of the opinion that science must be made more useful as a resource for arriving at political decisions. As governor of New York, Roosevelt opposed the idea of scientific economic research in the service of government. But now, according to Moley, "we have moved towards developing ideas and measures that are completely outside our representative system of government and to the place where legislative bodies become only a rubber stamp to set such new measures in motion."

It was through Moley's efforts that Professor Rexford G. Tugwell joined the Brain Trust as well. Professor Tugwell is not the only economic staff member but certainly the most radical and influential one. According to Tugwell, the entire time of Hoover's administration was dangerously conservative and only concerned with solidifying privileges. Tugwell stands for drastic income and death taxes. He is in favor of the government taking over all essential companies if their profits are absorbed though taxation. He stands for nationalizing the banks and considers it entirely possible to eliminate the whole private banking system and sees such a measure received with great approval by the people. Primary among Tugwell's deliberations is the thought of increasing purchasing power and this becomes the hallmark of the Roosevelt agenda. With unequivocal directness, Tugwell summarizes the issues as follows:

> *Once the purchasing power fails, everything fails. If we have purchasing power, we have everything valuable leading to a genuine prosperity. But an increase in the purchasing power is not reached by waving a magic wand as many seem to believe; neither is it an obscure mystery that human agency is powerless on its own. That leaves one way – money must be taken from where it is found and redistributed where it should be. The remedy is a brutal and merciless taxation of*

the nation in order for government generously to supply consumers with enough money for the essential purchases necessary to restart the stalled engine. In this way, the source of income is renewed and the purchasing power reestablished. We should not waste our innovative spirit searching for false remedies to restore our power. We should not exhaust ourselves in a vain quest to restore confidence. Let us instead solidify our purchasing power once more.

Besides Moley and Tugwell, the Brain Trust includes young professors such as Law Professor, Adolf Berle, Jr. advocating for the extension of government control over business. How far the influence of the professors will touch the affairs of the country will become apparent later in the Roosevelt administration. Naturally, the affected parties feel threatened by such ideas as Tugwell's and voice deep misgivings about the Brain Trust. But on the other hand, the American public is burning the idols of yesterday, the captains of industry, leaders of commerce and great and small Babbitts (Sinclair Lewis' novel, *Babbitt*, 1922) who have fallen into deep discredit. The former slogans no longer avail. The American people are finished with the leaders who have governed America for the past decade with nothing but practical reason and have left a pile of rubble behind. When Roosevelt speaks of his plans for the country, he works in phrases such as "I have had a vision" and "I dream that someday, our country..." and the country delights in Roosevelt being able to dream as opposed to leaders who hide the poverty of their ideas behind a corpulence of initiatives while still promising the average citizen better times with red faces and affable smiles. The American people encourage the contemptuously treated professors to step forward now. It is one of the most remarkable sociological shake-ups in the history of the United States. The average American imagines three caps to be always hanging on the clothes stand in Roosevelt's dressing room with the president saying to himself, "Let's give the professors a chance!"

Roosevelt announces his work projects.

Roosevelt visiting one of the camps he established.

The weekend president.

Roosevelt surrounded by family.

SIX

The Dawn of a New Era

It is clear, the solution is not to be found in everyday politics or in last minute remedies but in getting to the source of the evil.

—FRANKLIN D. ROOSEVELT

WHAT IS KNOWN ABOUT this person, Franklin D. Roosevelt, when he takes the oath of office and direction of the country for the next four years into his own hands? He has one of the most famous names in America and it is therefore unnecessary first to learn how to spell this name. People know the campaign about his inexhaustible energy and they admire the way he has conquered a difficult struggle with polio. Roosevelt's soft radio voice is recognizable by all, along with his hearty laugh and amazing blue eyes that can alternate between being wise, kind, and youthfully mischievous. He can be like a child among children, a trait appreciated by many. There are countless touching stories about the devotion of the paralyzed children at Warm Springs to their "First Crusader." Warm Springs sent a special train full of boisterous paralytics, who refuse to be labeled as cripples, to the Inauguration in Washington; they wanted to be present when one of their own accepted the highest office a nation can offer.

Roosevelt's personal courage is well known, too. During an earlier assassination attempt which struck the mayor of Chicago instead of the intended target, Roosevelt showed proof of such personal courage. He is always open to advice, does not claim to know better than others or aim to do everything himself. Many of those who pursue Roosevelt with the intention of questioning him are quickly the ones questioned instead by the newly elected president who exhibits a genuine interest in the other person and that individual's experiences. On the other hand, it is also known that Roosevelt might cut boring conversations with obtrusive visitors quickly. His curt reply to the New York Pastor, John Haynes Holmes, and the well-known Rabbi, Stephen S. Wise, when the two tried to tie Roosevelt to certain promises in the Jimmy Walker Affair, is often quoted. "If these critics just serve their God as they seek to serve themselves, the people of New York will become the beneficiaries," Roosevelt reflected dryly. But on another occasion, no one appeared more pitiful before Roosevelt than Mayor Jimmy Walker when Roosevelt finally resolved the Jimmy Walker Scandal in a calm and fundamental way.

Furthermore, Roosevelt has a sense of humor. The claustrophobic, two-minute silence that occurs on every American radio station before a presidential address might suddenly be interrupted with a mischievous comment, "Now listen, if someone needs to sneeze, please do it now." At Hyde Park, another reporter unexpectedly approached Roosevelt and when it was too big an effort to answer another political question, Roosevelt simply took the reporter to his farm and arranged a competition for the two to milk some cows. And at the recently installed movie theater in the White House, Roosevelt requests a Mickey Mouse feature whenever he attends.

It is generally known that Roosevelt has a deeply felt appreciation for everything human. As unrelenting as he might be with himself, he can be equally forgiving of others. The human individual is always at the center of his considerations. He does not seek political office simply for the sake of some theoretical reasons for reform but because the realities of poverty and the exploitation of others are distressful to his human sensibilities. By the end of his presidential campaign, Roosevelt wrote the touching human vignette:

The campaign was one long and disturbing experience. Today, no one can cross our continent and return home unchanged. I saw the situation as far worse than I had expected. I have looked thousands of Americans in the eye and in them I have found the faces of people living in abject poverty. I do not mean only the unemployed. Naturally they would have to accept the situation. But I mean those who still have work and are unsure of for how long. They carry the frightened expression of lost children. And I do not mean only bodily destitution. There is more. I was in Paris when Woodrow Wilson went to Versailles and I observed the crowds in the streets of Paris. In them I saw, especially in the faces of the women, the same expressions as I find in America today. It is a kind of longing... At that time, the French thought back on the war that had just ended. Perhaps this man can save our children from the tremors and fright which we have experienced, their eyes seemed to hope. Today the eyes of our fellow citizens are saying, We are caught up in something we do not understand. Hopefully this man can still rescue us.

Roosevelt fails. People make allowances for his human foibles. He is considered a good fellow. Yet, exceptional energy, courage and persistence are also expected of him. His stubbornness is well known from the political campaign. Moreover, years of illness have toughened him. Warm Springs is not a place to award momentary success or to crown a life with cheap laurels but to fortify the traits of a whole person. After having been in the tomb for years awaiting the other side to wear out, Roosevelt comes forth prepared to lead a war for jobs. He has reserves of strength stored up for the task.

Everyone senses this about Roosevelt. But less known are his spiritual convictions and the background for the ideas which he will announce as the New Deal. The final success of his efforts is going to depend on a spiritual foundation. Many hear nothing but pure demagoguery in his ideas. There are even prophets who prophecy that undoubtedly Roosevelt as president will to be more popular than his predecessor, but just as hated within six months.

The speed of change which takes place following Roosevelt's move to the White House leaves no time for theoretical discussions. The country has no choice but to accept the extensive and thoroughly revolutionary legislative agenda. Theoretical questions of whether Roosevelt is the right man for change or not are quickly overshadowed by the events of the day. As he stood on the steps of the Capitol on March 4th, Roosevelt asked for full authority to fight the Depression as in a time of war. Then, on March 6th he announced a national bank holiday; on March 9th Roosevelt presented Congress with emergency bank legislation to be implemented immediately; on March 10th he requested a savings authorization from Congress to relieve the federal budget of eight hundred million dollars through a fifteen percent cut in the salaries of every federal employee and a revision of the pension for veterans. Less than a week later, on March 11th the House of Representatives adopted the savings authorization and on the same day, Roosevelt issued an order for the gradual reopening of the banks. On March 13th the President requested Congress for the immediate resumption of the production of beer; on March 14th the House of Representatives passed this legislation and on March 15th the Senate passed the savings authorization.

This is how the government proceeded for the next four months until the end of June and it is only after all the important legislative work was wrapped up that the special session of Congress adjourned for summer vacation. Members of Congress returned home believing they had worked through the country's most serious hours. Roosevelt succeeded in jump-starting the legislative machine and after the Hoover administration's long years of lethargy, the speed and efficiency of the new legislative agenda are acceptable to the public-at-large. The country takes notice of the legislative whirl of activity in Washington and grants the new president its enthusiastic approval.

Perhaps Roosevelt will have to revise many of the decisions later, but for the present, a wrong directive is better than no direction at all. The last four months have taught America this lesson. Furthermore, the most important laws pushed through by Roosevelt are laws of empowerment that help make the surgery more bearable and that allow for a retreat later if necessary. Roosevelt has generally operated in the past with caution in using empowerment, the example being with currency production. But the Democratic majority in both Houses now moves forward in lockstep with the president. If the tempo were to slow, strong opposition is certain to rise up against him. But the opposition stays disorganized and weakened by the pace of change. With or without authorization, Roosevelt enforces his will unrestrictedly. Congress is left in a bind by his proposals and both Houses are reduced to passing insignificant, unimportant attachments or legislative amendments.

The majority of Roosevelt's ambitious plans that weekly surface from his repository were first conceived through serious discussions with the Brain Trust before Roosevelt even took office. Many are the result of yearlong studies. After the election, in the period between November and March, Roosevelt definitely refused to make political compromises with Hoover and stayed adamant about getting a head start to his presidency. The public and government both subject themselves to Roosevelt's powerful leadership. "In every trying hour of our national life, strong and honest leadership has enjoyed the understanding and support of the people. Such support is essential for victory and I am convinced that Congress will have the people's support in these critical days as well."

The press feels drawn into the confidence of Roosevelt. There is the same informality with the press as always in Roosevelt's presence, and now press conferences even take place in Roosevelt's private office. He is convinced that every reporter in Washington will introduce him personally to the public and Roosevelt makes sure to develop a relationship and to shake each one's hand. The notorious, pre-issued, previous press-briefs full of official optimism are no longer available from the gatekeepers of the Hoover administration. During critical moments, Roosevelt uncovers his cards fully before the journalists, or at least gives the impression of doing so. He speaks from personal knowledge succinctly and concisely about any new measures that are planned and explains thoroughly the prerequisites and intentions of his policies. He demands the same process from his staff with the result that Roosevelt has come to enjoy excellent press coverage throughout the country and the former monotonous, official, optimistic forecasts of the optimists are replaced by a sincere optimism issued from the pens of the journalists instead.

Roosevelt is able in this way to pass laws that previously broke the backs of his predecessors. For example, the savings authorization was passed without precedent. Previous presidents certainly demanded similar authorization and received millions of public funds for distribution but it is unheard of for a president in American history to demand such an authorization, to reduce at his own discretion salaries and veterans' pensions in order to save eight hundred million dollars, and furthermore, to have the same authorization in his pocket five days later. Instead, memories linger of the Hoover White House besieged by war veterans, and of the grumbling throughout the country that followed when President Hoover dispersed the demonstrators and allowed the camps of veterans to be burned. Roosevelt completely ignores these shady experiences of his predecessor. He addresses the country about the irregularities in veterans' pensions and his plans for making major adjustments. The country moves with Roosevelt and there is no trainload of veterans heading for Washington in protest.

Roosevelt's ability to get authorization for a reduction in the federal budget affects state budgets as well. The governor of Indiana demanded and got authorization to cut his annual state budget by two to three million dollars and across the board a certain governmental fatigue with the American model of democracy is clearly recognizable.

At first, the Roosevelt legislation does not reach beyond the immediate emergency, such as the bank legislation, but it clearly signals efforts by the new administration to rebuild the economy on two fronts. The primary front is the restoration of the purchasing power for farmers through planned agriculture even if this means limitations on individual farmer's freedom. The second front is the restoration of the purchasing power for laborers and entrepreneurs in the cities by contracting them to certain norms under the price of economic freedom.

The farm issue is the first to be addressed by Roosevelt, not because the need is the greatest here or because he, too, is a farmer. No, he is genuinely concerned about farming, and will most likely continue to lobby for the farm, because he sees the future of the nation in the land. He does not believe in increasing the concentrations of industry or in the inevitable growth of giant cities. He does not have faith in a Tower of Babel but hopes the open countryside will be rediscovered, cities vacated, and that city dwellers will bring with them what is most attractive about living in the cities.

The first farm legislation emanating from Roosevelt's desk includes emergency measures as well as fundamental statutes. A restraining order was issued that will protect farmers from farm foreclosures, such foreclosures as were already instituted during the Hoover administration and that led to farmer revolts. Courts were prevented from carrying out the foreclosures by threats and powerful opposition, but when they were carried out under military protection, local farmers in solidarity with each other hindered the measures from being put into effect. In protest, a neighbor might repossess the foreclosed farm for a few cents and give it back to its rightful owner.

Those unhappy situations for debtors and creditors alike are now stopped through an act of funding and the federal government has made two billion dollars available for this purpose. Creditors of imperiled farm mortgages receive the right by law to exchange farm mortgages for a four percent federal debenture bond. The farmer becomes a debtor of the federal government and his interest burden is determined at four and a half percent. There is a danger for the government, however, that it will become overwhelmed with bad mortgages; the debtor becomes reasonably happy but no creditors will consider exchanging his high interest mortgages for low interest bonds.

The second and more serious concern is the price ceiling in agriculture and how again to lift it to a level that will enable farms to survive. A devaluation of the dollar is not sufficient in itself; special measures must to be taken to save the farm so that production and needs are brought into equitable balance.

Various factors led to the agricultural surpluses in the first place. Originally, new farm technology caused the overproduction. It worsened during the Depression due to lowered consumption by the unemployed. Furthermore, the export market suffered from the overseas markets shutting down. The Hoover Administration's only remedy was to purchase the overflow which further increased the amount of unsold, warehoused agricultural products, especially wheat and cotton. Warehousing depressed the price of goods even further. Meanwhile, farmers happily continued to produce new surpluses as they reasoned, "The government will buy them from us."

As long as consumption remained low, there was no other alternative than radically to reduce cultivation. No farmer willingly did the logical thing without the fear of the law's enforcement on his back. When an ad campaign for the reduction of cotton production aired on the radio, every farmer believed his neighbor would be dumb enough to listen to the voice of the government. Thus if all neighbors reduced their production, the price of cotton would have to go up again, the individual farmer reasoned, with the result that farmers even plowed their vegetable gardens in order to plant more cotton. The advertising campaign led to greater harvests than before. Prices fell even further. In the end, forty-five percent of the wheat harvest could no longer be accommodated on the domestic market.

It is at this point that Roosevelt introduces a drastic program for farm relief. For the wheat grower, forty-five percent of land must lie fallow and in return, Roosevelt guarantees the prewar price for the rest of the farmer's yield. In the event that this prewar price cannot be reached, the government will commit itself to pay the difference in cash. In many cases the farmer will also be free to lease parcels of fallow land to the government in return for money. With the cotton crop, growers must commit themselves to destroying one third of all their seedlings. In return, they will receive the right to government warehouse facilities. Then, with an anticipated increase in prices, growers will again be able to earn both from their own harvests and from their farm bureau reserves.

As paradoxical as it might sound, it is logical to promise the farmer a premium for working less. In order to keep the support of the middle of the voting public for the implementation of this unusual measure, the government promises to tax the primary users of agricultural products. From now on, the mill will have to carry the tax on grain, the slaughterhouse the tax on meat, the spinning wheel the tax on cotton, the cigarette manufacturer the tax on tobacco and so on.

Another measure even more typical of Roosevelt's thinking, yet only indirectly applicable to the farm but one that will affect its future most broadly is the Tennessee Valley Project. The Tennessee Valley is an area of 640,000 square miles, larger than Germany's state of Bavaria and it is to be developed according to Roosevelt's new economic thoughts in a way similar to the German industrial development of East Prussia but on an American scale. As a first step, Roosevelt envisions the project to embrace reforestation along with the construction of dams and water power stations. The following goals will be pursued: the flood regulation of the Mississippi River, reclamation for agricultural use of the fertile lowlands now constantly suffering from seasonal flooding, divulgence of unfruitful acreage for reforestation and improved water flow, and provision of cheap power to the Tennessee area for the decentralization of industry.

This last item is one of the main points of Roosevelt's project. The Tennessee Valley, often referred to as "The Ruhr of America" because of unusually rich mineral deposits, is to experience new industrial development from the delivery of cheap electricity. An agricultural standard of living will be advanced and improved simultaneously with the creation of "agricultural/industrial" footholds. Such footholds are not meant to benefit agriculture alone but are intended to establish semi-farms where homesteaders might be able to raise a few chickens, perhaps a cow, grow vegetable gardens and harvest a few potatoes. As in East Prussia, these agricultural/industrial footholds are to be located adjacent to small cities or villages where some industries, perhaps a saw mill, paper factory or even a mine, will be operating.

Roosevelt had tried this model already when he was governor of New York and, according to Professor Moley, these trials had achieved generally good results. Out of fifteen unemployed families settled on a landed commune in New York State only one family had failed to gain a foothold.

Contrary to Roosevelt's intentions, however, the same arguments voiced in Germany against the industrialization of East Prussia are heard in America also. When Germans ask, "Why do we need new industry?" Americans ask, "Why do we need more farmers?" Roosevelt is not interested in creating a larger farm population, which in turn will only further increase farm surpluses, but in creating a new subgroup of laborers more likely to pull their own weight and meet their own needs.

Roosevelt comes up with a new ad campaign to decentralize industry, but the campaign ends up dividing the public's mind.

Henry Ford embraces the campaign with enthusiasm, however, and brings back an earlier, cherished plan of his own. It is probably an aspect of an industrial leader's personality to have strong political instincts also. Henry Ford kept this political instinct mute while he inserted himself with every available resource in the reelection campaign of Herbert Hoover. But after Roosevelt's victory, Ford just as happily embraces the opportunity to go in a new direction. In the future, he plans to "decentralize" his automobile factories. The chassis of a car can be produced from numerous agricultural byproducts and in his own words, "the chassis can grow from the acres." Ford wants motors to be produced in the central manufacturing plant in Detroit but have every chassis built in something like 50,000 small factories scattered around the country. And the various parts of a car shall be assembled in a dozen or so regional plants. Laborers will be able to spend half their days as farmers with their wages only to serve as a subsidy for the purchase of luxuries and the sale of such to profit the entire region.

The Alpha and Omega of the entire Tennessee Project will be the delivery of cheap electricity. The federal government has already operated a power station and nitrogen plant in the Tennessee basin, a situation that has been the subject of endless debate in Congress. But once the government turned the management of both the generation of electricity and it's delivery to consumers over to a private company, the Muscle Shoals Power Station became useless to the public. The company drew electricity from the state at the rate of one cent for five kilowatts per hour but delivered the same electricity to the consumer at not less than forty cents for five kilowatts per hour. Thus en route from producer to consumer, the price multiplied forty times.

Roosevelt wants to put an end to this situation and to give to the state the responsibility for the production and distribution of electricity. In a speech to Congress, he requested the acceptance of the Tennessee project and insisted on establishing a Tennessee Valley department to function like a corporation, vested with the authority of the government, possessed with the flexibility and initiative of private enterprise and, through careful planning in the widest sense of the word, entrusted with the management of the Tennessee basin for its appropriate use and natural preservation. Roosevelt sees the Tennessee project as just the first attempt at regional economic planning with the same principles to be applied later to other areas of the country and finally, to the entire nation.

In order to start work immediately in the Tennessee Valley and on similar projects elsewhere, Roosevelt establishes a new volunteer labor force, called the Civilian Conservation Corps, and within three months an army of 275,000 men was mobilized to work across the continent in 1,200 different locations. Most recruits, however, flood to the Tennessee area. With such an army of workers, organized and supervised under the strict jurisdiction of army officers and overseen by the Minister of Labor, Francis Perkins, extensive forest clearings are ready to begin in earnest. Roads and paths will be created simultaneously through the immense forest areas enabling more effective control of forest fires and tree epidemics. Such efforts in many cases signal the first economic inroads into primeval forests.

The call to the Civilian Conservation Corps is entirely voluntary but the responses repeatedly far surpass available employment opportunities. Therefore, only volunteers recommended for work by their welfare agencies are accepted. One requirement for placement is that volunteers have needy dependents and live in areas where welfare services are overwhelmed by too heavy caseloads. Willing recruits receive thirty dollars a month from which about twenty-five dollars are returned to their dependents. In this way, the left hand of the public saves what the right hand safeguards.

The Civilian Conservation Corps resembles the German labor corps only slightly. It misses the integration of diverse social groups, which is considered an essential part of the German effort. American volunteers are exclusively sought from poor areas, especially the immigrant quarters of the big cities. In place of camaraderie, military discipline is strictly enforced. Little attention is given to the important question of leisure activities. Newspapers announce broadly whenever ten to twenty thousand new recruits have been accommodated and their numbers are suddenly considered provided for, rescued from misery as if snatched from the jaws of wretchedness. The public is satisfied. Wherever possible, the rich still donate Sunday chicken dinners to such work camps. But workers begin to grumble in their free time. They do not understand the actual nature of the work. Planned forestry is a new concept in America. Whenever in the past someone wanted to hunt even a raccoon seeking refuge in a tree, then, for the sake of simplicity, half the tree was simply cut down; no one found anything odd about this except the raccoon. But now that Roosevelt wants to plant new trees in every clearing, at least he should be willing to pay an honest salary such as is paid for decent work everywhere else. This is the argument heard among the Conservation Corps and frequent mutinies and strikes are the result.

Trade unions also vigorously fight the Civilian Conservation Corps. They interpret it both as a modern form of slavery and a competitive danger to well-paid work. Opposition to this "un-American" arrangement reaches deep into the middle class. The conservation corps nevertheless survives as a necessary part of Roosevelt's economic policy and is expected in due time to meet his agenda: "We will not plant trees alone. We will strengthen men."

The opposition from unions is also aimed at farm aid whenever it leads to higher prices for consumption. Such opposition is first muted once Roosevelt widens his attack on poverty on every front, including an assault on working conditions within the industrial sector as well.

The first attack on the industrial front is Roosevelt's effort at the alleviation of the most severe poverty. Already during Roosevelt's first weeks in office, 500 million dollars for direct help with unemployment were appropriated. It is important to note that this money will not flow exclusively to those in need through the former channels of private charity organizations, but will also be allocated to the self-help organizations that have arisen during the Depression such as the centers for bartering that now appear in many parts of the country. Frequently voiced theoretical reservations remain unspoken at this time; priorities are shifting to the movement of fast and effective relief to those crisis situations where eking out an existence is growing as if organically from the soil.

The second Roosevelt offensive on the industrial front is a public jobs creation program on an unprecedentedly large scale and three and a half billion dollars have been made available for this purpose. Two thirds of this vast sum will be designated for use by the individual states and municipalities; public corporations will receive thirty percent of the total as a write-off from the federal government and the remainder at unusually generous terms. The purpose is to expedite a rapid and effective economic recovery. However, here opposition is also encountered. Budget Director, Lewis Douglas, only wants the money to enter the economy in small doses while Professor Tugwell of the Brain Trust worries that a too cautious use of the money will fail to stimulate the public works program. The clash between these two men is similar to an earlier clash in convictions between Raymond Moley and Cordell Hull, resulting in Moley's retirement from the State Department as is generally known.

Roosevelt's decisive third thrust is his initiative to raise wages and shorten the workday as promised earlier in his campaign. The first step is taken in the middle of April when, with the persuasion of Roosevelt, the governor of New York, Herbert H. Lehman, pushes the state to pass a minimum wage law. President Roosevelt seizes the opportunity and sends a telegram to the governors of all the principal industrial states – New Jersey, Pennsylvania, Connecticut, Rhode Island, Illinois, Indiana, Ohio, Michigan,

Maryland, Delaware, North Carolina, Alabama and New Hampshire – directing their attention to the recently passed New York law and encouraging them to pass similar statutes.

Roosevelt's appeal to the individual states, entitled according to the Constitution to social legislation, did not generate the anticipated results. Roosevelt nevertheless moved ahead and led the federal government in the initiative that became known as the National Industrial Recovery Act. This legislation passed on June 17th and with its passage, the most productive session of Congress is concluded. The National Industrial Recovery Act represents the high point to date of Roosevelt's legislative accomplishments.

It is important to note that Roosevelt's many proposals pulled from his desk drawer during these months passed both Houses of Congress without serious opposition. They include rulings on inflation, the authorization for an additional distribution of three billion dollars in bank notes, a reduction of the federal budget, aid to railroads and farmers, bank legislation and even the Muscle-Shoals statute, the latter breaking precedent as it suggests a new transition toward a government-planned economy. But with the National Industrial Recovery Act, Roosevelt for the first time confronts real opposition from both Houses of Congress and the opposition is in large part supported by the capitalist press. The liberal international presses, including Germany's, do not raise their warning voices against socialist experimentation. In Germany, however, the echo reverberating through a great forest of printed pages is not melodious but fearful. Could such dangerous "Hussar tricks" perhaps be translatable to other countries as well?

Many items of the National Industrial Recovery Act resemble the amendments on cartels passed by the German Reich Cabinet in July. The German amendments are to be enforced by the German Minister of Economic Affairs, but in the American statute, their enforcement will fall under the jurisdiction of the President or his representatives. While price points are at the center of the German legislation, working conditions are in the forefront of Roosevelt's law. Industrial norms are to be established by voluntary agreements of employers of certain industries with "fair competition" to be the binding principle on each particular industry. The minimum wage and maximum work week must meet certain standards, but fixed prices and conventional penalties will not be introduced. Instead, the President will link his governing bodies to all the amendments, including the implementation of punishment for breaches of contract, and a system of licensing will be enforced on outsiders to exclude them from business.

With the National Industrial Recovery Act Roosevelt overturned the entire existing legislation on cartels. His uncle, Theodore Roosevelt, first introduced the Anti-Trust laws meant to protect consumers from monopolies and to anchor unfettered competition in law. The textile industry, however, became an example of where such a principle could lead certain industries. At this time of general unemployment, the United States Women's Bureau reports that there still are seamstresses in the state of Connecticut who work sixty-four hours per week. In other cases, textile industries relocate to states with laws that make room for the widest margin in the exploitation of women and children, and today there are still places in Kentucky where the wage is only thirty-five cents for an eight hour workday, the result of unfettered competition.

From now on, Roosevelt tethers both the employer-employee relationship and the prevention of murderous competition to law. He hopes to serve not only the interests of the worker but also to reach a general, steady increase in purchasing power. This becomes the most contentious point in Roosevelt's stimulation of the economy. With the anticipation of further inflation and higher wages, industry expands production in such speculative ways that increases in total wages fail to approximate the same ratio. Between March and June, 1933, industrial production based on 1923 to 1925 figures increased from sixty to eighty-nine percent of the normal output, employment grows only from fifty-seven to sixty-five percent and total wages from thirty-seven to forty-six percent. The possibility of another dangerous collapse lies herein.

Once the law passed, the opposition took a wait-and-see attitude. What will the implementation of the law look like in practice? Even within Roosevelt's own party the opposition makes itself heard. This new direction has socialist aspects about it. Once more, Alfred E. Smith distances himself from Roosevelt as well and writes the following in his paper, *The New Outlook* in July:

> *If the regulations in this new law are carried out verbatim, it will undoubtedly lead to private initiative being crippled, monopolies being legally anchored and officially supported, prices being increased and higher tariffs imposed to maintain the new design. Thus in a triumph of bureaucracy the small individual will be lost. These new regulations do not need to be applied. They will just create an opportunity for radicals to introduce a new vehicle and leave the servicing of the vehicle to reactionaries. In the end, neither group will be satisfied. It has nothing to do with the traditional politics of the Democratic Party, from the time of Thomas Jefferson the party against centralized government and the party for the individual, for individual States rights and private initiative. Personally, I favor limits on industry where necessary but I am not for placing the heavy, crippling hand of government on the entire economic life of our nation. I believe in good, administrative management but also in knowing its limits. I am for the restoration of conditions that enable economic leadership and against the expectations that such leadership will come from the government.*

The American economy is restructured and President Roosevelt becomes chairman of the National Recovery Council, the top economic body that meets regularly every week. Roosevelt has five direct reports on the council, 1) the National Industrial Recovery Administration, 2) the Emergency Public Works Administration, 3) the Agricultural Adjustment Administration, 4) the Tennessee Valley Authority, and 5) the Federal Coordinator of Transportation.

- The National Industrial Recovery Administration, under the chairmanship of General Hugh Johnson, makes sure the codes of industry and trade are implemented.

  The Reconstruction Finance Corporation or Credit Union established by Herbert Hoover, reports directly to the NIRA and is also chaired by General Jones.

- The Emergency Public Works Administration with a budget of 3.5 billion dollars implements the creation of new public works.

  The Federal Emergency Relief Administration reports directly to the Public Works Administration and has more than 500 million dollars at its disposal for direct unemployment assistance.

- The Agricultural Adjustment Administration manages the Farm Relief Program and distributes bonuses for farmers limiting the cultivation of arable land.

  The Federal Farm Credit Administration provides funding for farmers and

  The Federal Home Loan Bank Board funds needy, municipal single home owners equivalent to the funding for farmers.

- The Tennessee Valley Authority becomes the top department for planning and developing the Tennessee Valley.

The Civilian Conservation Corps falls under the jurisdiction of the TVA and is responsible for employment in reforestation and similar projects.

- The Federal Coordinator of Transportation, also the commissioner for the railroad companies, is equipped with dictatorial authority over all transportation.

Roosevelt does not for one moment leave the country in the dark. He considers the National Industrial Recovery Act the cornerstone of his legislation and immediately dedicates himself to its realization. He names General Hugh Samuel Johnson to be the administrator of industrial recovery and requests industry urgently to present statutes of fair competition. General Johnson is perfect for the job. During the War, he accepted on behalf of the country the entirely new task of organizing an army of one million men. And after the war, he entered industry. He lacks nothing in the way of experience or success and therefore is perfectly suited for the position now. Furthermore, the cantankerous general likes to have final authority over co-workers and negotiating partners alike, such as professors, entrepreneurs and trade union leaders.

In some cases agreement is not easily reached. The statute for the textile industry triggers enthusiastic applause when first adopted, signed and set in motion by Roosevelt. The president of the Association of Cotton Industries announces in a dramatic meeting with labor representatives and the government commissioner the Association's decision to stop employing children under the age of sixteen. From the time of the establishment of the textile industry more than a hundred years ago, child labor had been a requirement for competition. No employer who wanted to stay competitive would have considered relinquishing the statute, which is now suddenly eliminated with the stroke of a pen. Within three months, change in the adult labor law must also be carried out. The work week is to be set at a maximum of forty hours and the minimum wage to be established at twelve dollars for Southern states and thirteen dollars for Northern states. Social reformers have fought a futile fight against child labor in the United States for decades when an amendment forbidding child labor should have been passed long ago. But in the past, only four or five out of the forty-eight states were ready to accept such an amendment that required at least thirty-six states to pass. Now overnight, child labor is eliminated by a minimum wage act which makes child labor no longer profitable.

Agreement is not always reached that quickly, however. A distributor of colonial products presents a statute that, for example, envisions a fifty-four hour week with a salary scale of twelve to sixteen dollars for males and nine to eleven dollars for female employees with salaries to be one dollar lower in the Southern states. Likewise the steel industry on several occasions presents statutes that must be rejected again and again as insufficient.

Roosevelt and General Johnson emphasize repeatedly that what concerns them most is to facilitate an increase in purchasing power in order to speed a rise in prices and production, if not at least to keep pace with them. A decline in purchasing power must under no circumstances come from enlarging the work force. When Roosevelt first announced the National Industrial Recovery Act on June 16, 1933 he made the following points:

I am aware that an increase in wages might possibly elevate the costs of production but I am requesting employers first and foremost to consider improving employee benefits while awaiting an increase in sales such as is sure to follow with the purchasing power of the population increasing. Such a consideration correlates with good business sense and the national economy. Our efforts aim for the restoration of the domestic market and for the great power of consumption to grow again. If we raise prices at the same speed as salaries, the whole plan will be worthless. We can only hope that our plan will succeed if we postpone price increases during these critical months as long as possible even at the cost of profits to industry.

Historically, there has always been considerable opposition to economic policies that aim to raise purchasing power in capitalist countries. Such opposition also exists in the United States. Every attempt at encouragement by General Johnson and the Commander in Chief is understated and those most directly affected hear nothing. However, when the energetic general announces the implementation of basic regulations for all industries and the plan fails to generate even passive opposition, industry takes notice. A major attack on Roosevelt follows.

This latest attack is meant to strike Roosevelt at the price point, the most vulnerable point of his economic policy. Roosevelt sees the hoped-for impetus for his measures in the rising costs of raw materials. To strike Roosevelt, it is not enough for securities to plummet from their heights – no one denies that speculation drove securities to unjustifiable heights in the first place – but the price of raw materials, especially of agricultural products, must be brought down, so as to separate Roosevelt from his strong farm following. That is exactly what happened the third week of July on the American Stock Exchange. A carefully promoted panic became a vivid reminder of another historic episode. To scrutinize these latest trading events, Roosevelt immediately appointed the New York Prosecutor, Ferdinand Pecora, who distinguished himself in earlier courageous actions against John Pierpont Morgan and other powerful forces of that day.

Roosevelt and his administration initiates a two-pronged counter attack. The first is to establish a minimum price for grain and to give the commodities exchange just a few cents of leeway in daily fluctuation. Of the entire world, the Soviet Union is the only one in the past to make such a radical break with the principle of free trade. But before any other priorities, this Compulsory Statute is adopted. The mailman delivers a letter from the White House on July 27th, addressed to every employer, in which Roosevelt invites the employer to secure with him a contract guaranteeing a minimum wage, the work week and limited price inflation. Employers are asked to sign and return the contract to the President immediately wherever possible. The contract will be implemented on August 1st. Roosevelt simultaneously issues the Seal of the Blue Eagle to all who sign the contract with him. Employers are encouraged to wear and attach the Blue eagle to all their products. Forcing a signature is not possible according to the Constitution but the pressure of public opinion is even more effective. The means used here are the same that were used in 1917 in signing the war loan. With masterful oratory Roosevelt addresses the nation:

I have no trust in some panacea but I do believe that we hold the economic power in our own hands. I have no trust in national economies that claim things must take their own course or that human actions have no influence over economic ills. I mistrust such simple answers. At the same time, I know that for decades national economies have changed their economic laws every five or ten years.
I maintain my trust in the effectiveness of our common goals and in the power of the American people, united in action.

Therefore, I request all employers to sign this contract with me in the name of patriotism and humanity. And for the same reason I request all workers to join in the march with us, united in spirit, understanding and support.

The appeal works. The White House is flooded with statements of support. Many employers sign the blank regulations immediately in order to be the first among those who earn a place on the honor roll and receive the Blue Eagle. The experiences of 1917 are recalled. A boycott can evolve overwhelmingly quickly. F. D., as Roosevelt's most enthusiastic followers now call him, rolls up his sleeves. All of Washington shifts into third gear to cope with the work quotas. The trustee for employment, General Johnson, races from conference to conference until his socks literally droop over his shoes.

The entire United States comes under the sign of the Blue Eagle with this appeal and the symbol is intended to bring six million people or half the country's unemployed back to work before winter.

The blank regulations are only meant to be an emergency measure for a short period of transition; they are to be changed into individual codes that address the unique needs of the various industries as soon as possible. Initially the hope is that the national economy can be organized into a dozen or so industries that will require a relatively small number of regulations. If the Big Five, coal, steel, oil, textile and automobiles, are brought into line then other industries will present no great obstacles, so the reasoning goes. Historically, however, economic individualism knows how to hinder more broad uniform developments. Even shirt button factories start to demand their own cartel statute and thousands of industries soon present their own demands to the National Recovery Administration. At first, only a few dozen regulations are signed and put into effect.

The same obstacles also emerge with the Big Five. Regulations, especially for the petroleum industry, create considerable problems and in the automobile industry, Henry Ford succeeds in staying entirely outside the compulsory cartel statute. Once more a fight erupts between the powerful politician and the no less powerful, autocratic leader of industry. The auto king refuses to sign the contract. Ford enjoys both the open and veiled support of all who yearn for the return of Herbert Hoover and the "healthy" principles of the Republican Party, and a group of partisans who wish the administration a public setback gathers around Henry Ford. The latter emphatically insists, however, that he is ready to lower the work week in his companies from forty to thirty-five hours and to adopt the code. He even offers to raise the minimum wage above the limits set by the code. The administration lets him run with it for the administration will surely be on the wrong side with the public if they insist on the entire code's implementation for Henry Ford. As far as production numbers, determined for the Ford Company according to the NRA code, they will still be achieved through competition even without Ford's collaboration. In the end, the auto king triumphs only in his strict anti-union posture. Here, Ford even refuses to speak to a union man.

Henry Ford wins publicity only in his "victory" over Roosevelt and perhaps that is all that matters for Ford. In 1929, he produced 1.3 million cars in the United States; in 1932, that number fell to just 262,000. His share of the American domestic market dropped from forty percent in 1930 to twenty-four percent in 1932 and registers only twenty percent in the first half of 1933. The Chrysler Corporation for the first time joins General Motors in surpassing Ford and the two automobile companies push the former number one to third place.

Even if Roosevelt is to succeed in moving the economic revolution forward, he will still encounter new cells of opposition. No sooner is an acceptable compromise reached with Henry Ford than a serious conflict breaks out with the banks. One of the biggest challenges for the National Recovery Administration is the stabilization of prices for companies at the same time as companies must carry the costs of increased wages and employment and wait until the resultant gain in purchasing power restores profitability once more. The transition is dependent on the availability of strong credit and here the banks find an opportunity to sabotage the Roosevelt program.

The banks maintain at first that requests for credit do not exist. This claim, however, is made on such weak grounds that not even the banks believe it. If there really is no demand for credit despite the temporary spike in the costs of production caused by the lack of rising yields, then after four years of a difficult depression, American industry ought to be decorated with an unprecedented certificate of health. The banks quickly correct themselves. Although there are those seeking credit, their requests do not involve the money market, i.e. banks, but rather the capital market, i.e. the investors. Banks, too, await new bond issues and therefore push the entire problem onto the dead platform of an asset-seeking American public.

The moment to intervene has arrived. Roosevelt sends the uninvited chairman of the Reconstruction Finance Corporation, General Hugh Jones, to the annual meeting of the American Bankers' Association in Chicago and here General Jones directs some encouraging remarks to the gathering of distinguished bankers. The administration will take over the leadership of the banks. Bank presidents will simply become errand boys if their banks refuse voluntarily to support the NRA program with generous lending from their sizable liquidities. In conclusion, General Jones presents the convention with a resolution. The banks will sell their preferred shares to the government and their place and voice in the administration will be removed. The resolution must be adopted unanimously without opposition. The banks are brought into line and financing for the transition guaranteed.

While the pages of this book are going to press, a verdict cannot be made yet on the final success of the Roosevelt policies. Hand in hand with the challenges, the will of the administration to tackle the challenges is also growing. What an English journalist has said about Roosevelt for months now seems correct, "There is fighting blood in the Roosevelt clan. Perhaps an earlier tenacity will resurge in the same blood now coursing through the arteries of the new President. If he does choose the more arduous path, he will have more opportunities than any president since Abraham Lincoln and, it might be added, posterity honors the man who chooses the more difficult path."

Roosevelt's opponents are poised to exploit every setback his policies might encounter. A leader of the Republicans, who does not want to be identified, has plainly voiced it in the New York Times. According to him, the Republican Party needs only keep watchful eyes on the Democrats to profit from their mistakes. The well known Republican, Ogden Mills, has already professed that the Republicans will stubbornly hold on to their beliefs. "Progress and prosperity," he says, "are the normal conditions of American life. I see the future of the United States not as a country with fewer factories but with more, not with less industry but with more, not with a limited production of goods but with a continued, steady, rapidly expanding production line."

If the economic conditions improve under Roosevelt's leadership, the prophets of the other party will claim that the economic conditions would have lifted faster and more broadly under a Republican president employing healthier, traditional economic principles. It makes sense for Roosevelt to act quickly to stop the inflation. If another speculative expansion returns inevitably leading to new setbacks, the downsides of a stagnant economy must be clearly enunciated and prosperity based on economic booms and speculative profits renounced.

Roosevelt faces an enormous challenge here, a challenge primarily of an educational kind. Memories are still vivid in the minds of the American people of the boom times that lasted until 1929 and they expect every president now to restore the same prosperity, i.e. the prosperity of 1929. Roosevelt must preach a new definition of prosperity. Such a definition must be able to penetrate the minds and hearts of the people in the same way as the idea of "the common good" is starting to penetrate the Germans. The public ultimately is left paying the bill of every collapse and the public must be persuaded of a wiser course: to avoid such collapses in the first place.

Appendix A

Die Tagliche Rundschau, Berlin, April 27, 1933

A Fascist Roosevelt
By Helmut Magers

ROOSEVELT'S ASTONISHING speed of legislation makes it difficult for American correspondents in Washington to keep up with his pace. Draft legislations move from Senate to the House, amendments are railroaded through, presidential orders are issued, journalists rush from one press conference to another and every two or three days a new law is signed and sealed.

Such speed is already a phenomenon. Following the long stagnation of the Hoover years, the country demands this activity. Possibly, Roosevelt also makes questionable decisions that later have to be reversed, but a wrong decree is better than no direction at all. That principle applies today to America as well. Roosevelt's boldness sweeps the country. If he showed timidity, strong opposition would immediately form against him. He is in a fortunate position today of having an overwhelming majority of Americans with him as well as large majority in both houses of Congress. The underlying opposition is not organized, adding to its impotence. Therefore, with or without opposition Roosevelt's will is absolute. His proposals leave Congress as originally presented and for the time being, the work of Congress shrinks to writing insignificant amendments. It is the belief in Washington that a large part of Roosevelt's program will become law by the time Congress adjourns in the beginning of June.

The decisive element of Roosevelt's bluster lies in the fact that he has worked his plans out with a narrow circle of advisors before even being inaugurated. He has used the time since the election in November to make a strong start to his four year term. The majority of the proposals which Roosevelt almost daily pulls from his desk drawer come from years of preparation. Congress, as well as the American public, senses that they have strong leadership now and they are willing to follow. Because of the visit of European statesmen in Washington there is currently a break in the American legislative output. It allows for the scrutiny of the most recent proposals and it is relatively unimportant whether these proposals have been accepted by both houses already. It is the assumption that the unrevised proposals will certainly become law.

Apart from the currency bill proposing a partial, possible defrayment through silver, the most important recent measures are the approval of five hundred million dollars for direct unemployment assistance, the introduction of the thirty hour work week, and the creation of a labor force of 250,000 men, similar to the German labor service, to carry out charitable work. The revolutionary nature of the thirty hour work week must be seen in light of the fact that an eight hour day still was not law throughout every state. In many industries, especially the textile industry in the South, twelve to fourteen hour shifts were the norm. Against the opposition of certain states, now obligated through social legislation, the five day week and six hour workday is introduced though a federal measure. There are only a few exceptions for those who work in food companies, canned food factories, slaughter houses and industries dealing with perishable goods.

With the creation of the workers corps something like two percent of the unemployed will enter the workforce. The call to this corps is open to all young unemployed between eighteen and twenty five years of age. They must commit to one year's service but could be released if able to prove that they have a job to go to elsewhere. They will be employed primarily in clearing forests, flood regulations, and similar tasks to benefit the common good. They will receive benefits and full board in work camps arranged on the German pattern. There will be strong military discipline under the supervision of the military. The salary for the willing will be $30.00 per month. However, they are obligated to pass the biggest portion of this money on to their dependents and in this way, state funds for support will be relieved.

The American socialists label Roosevelt a fascist because of this labor corps. The description is not entirely absurd. Roosevelt brought out a book immediately after taking office which he proof-read already in the early days of March and provided the press with the book to coincide with his inauguration on March 4th. The book carries the optimistic title, *Looking Forward* and is published by John Day in New York. Ramsey MacDonald brings the book with him as reading material on his journey to America and is said to have remarked after finishing it, "Just like Hitler." Roosevelt's intention with the book is to outline the program for his four year term as president and details the circumstances which precipitated the book. The conclusion can be drawn that Roosevelt intends to be involved in every way and committed to a planned economy whereby the economic life of the country will no longer benefit just one small group of individuals but the whole population. "I believe that the future must be less about the producer and more about the consumer. The wage for one day's work has to be larger than before and for those working with capital, smaller."

Next, Roosevelt promises once more to bring the price of goods back to earlier rates. The first step in reaching this goal will be to establish gold parity for the dollar. Roosevelt speaks to the debt burden, especially that of agriculture, that it must be lowered but insists on keeping the consumer from being overcharged. The overproduction in agriculture of the last few years must be eliminated through a withdrawal of barren expanses of land from agricultural use. With the Agrarian Assistance legislation, announced April 12th, Roosevelt leads the way in restricting the land use for cultivation. Finally, Roosevelt suggests a far reaching redistribution of the population. He sees a third unit of the population, an agricultural – industrial subgroup, to augment the industrial and farming communities. This third group will work in industry without being proletarian and through the decentralization of industry, factories will migrate from the big cities to relocate on the flat stretches of land. The development of the Tennessee Valley in the meantime is approved as the first step in this direction.

The federal government has already for years operated a power station and a nitrogen plant in the Tennessee Valley. This power station at Muscle Shoals however has not been any less expensive to operate than private generation of electricity because a private company was called upon to run the power station and sell to the consumer. It ended up by monopolizing the distribution of electricity. The private concern paid the power station just one cent per five kilowatt hours of electricity and sold the same to consumers for forty cents. In the future, this situation will be rectified by the government taking charge of the generation of electricity as well as its distribution.

It is a shabby area of mismanagement when government officials who enact programs do not administer them properly. Roosevelt challenges these assumptions in his book wherein his path as statesman can be clearly followed. The book has an abundance of ideas to help the population in the twentieth century reach a common heritage. Will Roosevelt be a fascist, a national socialist or an American democrat? One would not be surprised if the United States, until recently the stronghold of capitalism, is further along on the way to socialism after Roosevelt's four year term in office.

Appendix B

Die Tagliche Rundschau, May 9, 1933

The Key Issue: Youth Pushing for Socialism
By Helmut Magers

Gleichschaltung – the elimination of all opposition – is a new word but not a new concept. Every revolution is followed by a time of *Gleichschaltung* – of bringing the opposition into line. And during revolutions, certain laws are eliminated. Despite fundamental differences in the sequence of political events in Germany, Italy and Russia, a number of parallels can still be found. In the first phase of these revolutions there was the seizure of power followed secondarily, by the reinforcement and implementation of that power, an event that in Germany is referred to as – *Gleichschaltung* – the elimination of all opposition. In the colorful, political language of Russia, this event was described as "a realignment of the highest commands." In the final phase, both Italy and Russia fused the party with the state.

From time to time, a nation's youth finds itself in the process of *Gleichschaltung* and eliminating all opposition. Within the German youth movement today, there is a lively discussion taking place about how practically to work out *Gleichschalting*. Out of necessity, united interests are still divided into associations and subgroups. Previously, youth would squander its energy while opposing the state. But every country that has been wiped out by a revolution has been a country run by an older generation. These states had failed to deal with its younger generation; led by its youth, oppositions formed and moved towards revolution when there was no role for them in the existing state. The need still exists to unite the youth, bring them into line and clarify what tasks the state will provide for them. Youth, who today heed the call to die for the national socialist movement and to carry it to victory, will still keep their eyes open for jobs after the struggle for complete power has been won. Even after the last trade union has been taken over and the last lending library been brought into line, the youth will confront the new state and demand a special role in it. And because currently, state and youth are welded together for the first time in German history, it will be easier to find new tasks for them.

How have other revolutions handled this problem? The Russian state placed its youth on the cultural and economic fronts. In the cultural area, the enormous task was to eliminate illiteracy in Russia. The cultural front in Germany is different. There is no illiteracy in Germany. But the whole German East presents a cultural front. Accordingly, in the service of borders Russian youth have been allowed on the cultural front. In the economic area, Russian youth have been engaged in the "bottlenecks" – bottlenecks such as occur with the harvest or at the coal-mining pits that fail to reach their targets. Thirdly, the military defense front has opened employment for the youth with both Italy and Germany rearming. However, the foundation that has inspired the youth in every area is the thought – it is about *our* country, *our* harvest, and *our* coal.

German youth has allowed itself everywhere to be infected with the fire of enthusiasm. Still, it must be remembered that youth and especially large numbers of German youth traditionally become uncivil and, as is the case most recently, anti-capitalist. The former revolutionary student songs, patriotic songs of the youth movement and camp songs of the S.A. (the Storm Troops) all strongly express this uncivilized spirit that clings to youth. They become ready to take up their positions in matters important to the people. Crowds of willing volunteers follow the call when a cry for help is heard

ROOSEVELT: A REVOLUTIONARY WITH COMMON SENSE

from one of the farmers or one of the villages. But they fold their arms when such help might benefit some larger estate. This happens in every area where the possibility for huge crowds and confrontation with the principles of capitalism present themselves and when it concerns labor or the housing market. From this point of view, *Gleichshaltung* or the elimination of all opposition by the youth is becoming the most important issue in the next phase of the German revolution. When the youth reject half of all the solutions offered, their demands become one of the strongest leverages for new socialist planning by the national socialist government.

Appendix C

Die Tat, an independent German monthly, July 1933.

Bridges to Roosevelt
By Helmut Magers

MANY SIMILARITIES EXIST between the United States and Germany today. The closer developments in America are observed since Roosevelt's ascent to office, the more similarities come into focus. However, Germans are more prone to make such comparative reflections than the Americans. For us, the United States includes an entire continent while in the American field of vision Germany is just one country among many in a rather confusing part of the world. Nevertheless, an awareness of parallelisms in developments might emerge over time and a convergence of interests find acceptance in the New World. It should be possible to achieve a friendly collaboration with the United States and excluding political differences, such collaboration would prove helpful to both countries.

In order to understand the present situation in the United States, the collapse of the last few years must first be explained. Roosevelt has begun to rebuild the economy on a field of rubble. The American phenomenon, that for the past decade so fascinated both the Western world and the American people, now lies in ruins. A holy doctrine promoted with Anglo-Saxon missionary zeal and meant to be spread to the entire world, turned out to be charlatanry; certainly the promotional efforts were no less intense than the promotion of the holy Russian doctrine of communism.

The American phenomenon with its spiritual supremacy no longer exists whereas the Russian phenomenon still does. Many who refused to fall for the Russian doctrine of salvation look to Germany now, located as it is between east and west, and wonder whether the birth of a new doctrine of salvation will be wrought there.

The dramatic rise and fall these last ten years in the New World must be recalled in order to discern on which side Germany stands today. America awakened to its destiny during the last War. A young nation found its vocation through its entry into the Great War and by shedding its blood, embraced the belief that it rescued the world from absolutism and imperialism. Concurrently, this nation experienced for the first time the unlimited possibilities for technical streamlining in production inherent in war. America's men were away for just eighteen months but that was enough time to usher in an enormous revolution in production.

Young men fit for service were primarily recruited from the countryside and with their conscription came the loud call for labor-saving farm equipment. The tractor industry especially credited the War for an unprecedented upturn in production. Of course there were tractors in operation already before the War. Some 80,000 were in use on the American farm by the end of 1917 but by the end of 1918, that number nearly doubled to 148,000. Tractors replaced both human and animal labor and worked more economically. This victory parade of tractors was therefore unstoppable in the time of peace and today the number of tractors on American farms has exceeded the first million. The Texas Agricultural Experiment Station has calculated that on a cotton farm of 200 acres, the total cost of production through the harvest with a tractor is $668.00 compared to $1,524.00 with the use of horse power. Even if the cost cannot be measured that exactly it can still be reduced by approximately half.

Along with the tractor, the harvester combine also revolutionized agriculture. The latter machine can both reap and thresh the grain in one cycle and it can chuck the corn into an attached tank. Already before the War, the harvester combine played a small role in the expansive wheat growing regions of the Northwestern states. To maneuver a prewar combine across the same expansive fields, it took a harness of up to thirty-six horses.

Today it takes just two men to drive a harvester combine. One day's performance with a medium combine equals to fifty or sixty mornings with the old-fashioned binding machine and twenty mornings now equal a good performance for two men. Thus the harvester combine has eliminated much of the need for the seasonal farm workers who in the past would migrate west with the harvest. However, the harvester combine is profitable mainly on certain large acreages of land; the minimum profitability of an average harvester combine with a span of 4.80 meters is approximately 300 acres. The maximum profitability for the same machine is reached on about 1,000 acres. The Kansas Agricultural Experiment Station has figured that for 500 acres of wheat, harvesting with a binding and free-standing threshing machine costs $4.41 per acre while the cost is $2.18 if using a harvester combine. In other words, the cost is cut in half.

Such facts have received a lot of attention in American agricultural circles. They have given much larger operations the advantage over smaller ones. As a result, the tendency has grown to enlarge the areas under cultivation. The price point on the wheat market gained an advantage while for small and middle-sized farmers the purchasing power kept falling. To stop such hemorrhaging, farmers took out mortgages freely offered, rationalizing that agriculture would continue to celebrate ever new triumphs, including even the electric milking of cows.

The death-knell of the capitalist economy can be found during these glowing years of *prosperity*. Professor Studensky-Moskau chronicles the effects of new agricultural technology in the United States in Volume 31 of the World Economic Archives and concludes as unavoidable the fact that the small capitalist middle class will be pulled away and the ranks of industrial wage earners swell. In another study, Dr. Charles Galpin of the Department of Agriculture, estimates migration from the land to have reached three million during the years of industrial bloom, 1920-1927.

Even during the good years in America there was certainly always some unemployment. The number of industrial laborers shrunk from 11.5 to 10.7 million following the streamlining of production and these figures included the ongoing influx of immigrants from other countries during the years, 1917-1927. At the same time, the number of individuals employed in commerce rose from 4.1 million to 6.1 million and in that area, the spirit of the age spoke most graphically. The American phenomenon rested essentially in the speed of the turnover of products.

The American post-war prosperity cannot be understood apart from the American style of high-pressure salesmanship. Long before the famous collapse in the autumn of 1929, all business, not only the stock market, took on a speculative character. Speculation was built into the fabric of the situation. America changed overnight during the war from being a debtor nation to becoming a creditor one. Enormous, available means pushed for both domestic and international investment. Such a phenomenon was first made possible with the opening of the continent and its borders. Industrial expansion suddenly seemed limitless so long as the market maintained the ability to soak up the extra production. A constantly escalating climate of lending sustained that ability for the market. It was nevertheless noticed relatively early that fostering and promoting production could not always stay in step with necessary increases in wages. Between the years, 1922-1927, production per laborer grew at an annual rate of 3.5 percent while the average wage rose only 2.4 percent. A dangerous development already showed itself here. Balance shifted from purchasing power and was further exacerbated by developments in the farm economy.

It is surprising how quickly such problems are sometimes overlooked. Prominent Americans earnestly believed they had found a perpetual forward momentum for the economy. Following a motto such as higher wages, greater turnover and growing profits, they believed that a depression could be warded off for all time. The phenomenon of overproduction did not exist in the imagination during those years. If limits for any market were finally reached, it was believed that extra production could always be off-loaded overseas. Exports would simply be financed by credit. If the question arose from whence the loans would be repaid, the joke of a moratorium was simply suggested.

Already in 1926, the first collapse threatened but the crisis was averted by a magic formula, an intervention that essentially contributed to the chronic and deep-rooted character of the current depression. This magic formula was the repayment/installment scheme. The commercial world hardly realized that the market situation was threatened by this balancing act and it did not catch wind of a coming catastrophe before it tried to stop the decline due to overproduction. The grandly perceived repayment scheme, whereby regular income of wage earners would be dragged along, became a means of maintaining a continuous stream of orders. With this formula, eyes were closed to the underlying causes of an approaching collapse.

If the crisis had broken out in 1926, it might still have worked itself through in the way of capitalism and have enabled links to a new economic system being made. But because declining economic activity was halted artificially against the warnings of reasonable economic and psychological minds, the whole scheme ballooned into suspended demands that came to burden even the smallest individual. At the outbreak of the crisis, an enormous amount of goods re-entered the trade after only short use and contributed to the collapsing market.

President Hoover's slogans on the campaign trail in 1928 read like a satire. For example, Hoover prophesied, "Prosperity is not empty word. It implies work for everyone. It means security and protection for every business and every home. And for current prosperity to continue, it is of utmost necessity to strengthen the politics of the Republican Party." Is it not the dream of a golden age, secured to the fifth generation that is promoted here? A well known American leader of industry, Edward U. Filene, who also chose not to be silent, at the same time penned these words, "Our new corporate culture has realized the socialist dream, albeit not by socialist means. For the first time in the history of humankind, leisure and luxury will be available for everyone and for the first time in the history of man, mass culture is in sight."

Such illusions have evaporated in the last three and a half years of crisis prior to the ascent of President Roosevelt. America is now ripe for the liquidation of the capitalist economic order wherein economic catastrophes such as the last Depression become inevitable; America is ready for new ways of healing. And this makes the current situation in the United States similar to the current German picture. Before all eyes, changes with unforeseeable consequences are being carried out in both countries. Politics always stands in the foreground in Germany; under the bold leadership of Roosevelt the United States marches by the way of economic restructuring. Most likely Roosevelt would resist being named a national socialist. And yet, it cannot be denied that his ideas have a resemblance to national socialist ideas. Roosevelt's socialism is not collectivistic. In his book he has repeatedly emphasized that he does not see his mission as saving American individualism. If he strengthens the state's control of economic life, as he intends to do, then this will protect the individual from being exploited by capitalist entrepreneurs and unscrupulous stockbrokers. Primarily, Roosevelt has started on a path leading to the inevitable end of the capitalist economic system. The more control by the state, the more the economy distances itself from the principle of individualism and turns in the direction of a progressive, forward-moving society. Roosevelt encounters closed opposition to reform for it is the opposition that has something to lose in a socialist economy. Even so, those for whom the economy has reversed itself stand unanimously by the President and that is today an overwhelming number of the American people.

We in Germany face the imperative to follow Roosevelt's actions closely and urgently for the German national socialist revolution will undoubtedly push towards similar economic developments. Experiences, shared between the two countries that have already begun in the work force, ought to be advantageous in the areas of economic restructuring as well. But in the political realm there also exists considerable confluence between the United States and Germany. Roosevelt's appeal to the people of the world for peace and Adolf Hitler's speech at the Reichstag open for the first time the possibility of political cooperation. And as the human family probably still faces a long time of redemption before any talk of disarmament, Germany might encounter American interests in this area, too.

Russia presents a second foreign policy moment. The recognition of Russia by the United States is possible in the foreseeable future. It could thus be assumed that America will honor its former intention of a Russian loan. An American loan would primarily promote American exports to Russia. It would furthermore eliminate Russia's dumping of products and would recapture the Russian market for the United States. Until now, America's business climate has shown itself favorable towards Russia. The consequences of Russia's talk regarding "speeding up" its huge, planned Soviet projects have elicited sympathy in the United States. Plus, the American export market to Russia held up with surprising vitality during the years of the Depression and in contrast to the developments in the rest of the world, could still be expanded and strengthened. Only the great risk inherent in a Russian loan being outside the letter of the law weigh against the reasonable economic considerations for such a loan. Great risks are usually left in every country to the state and between the years, 1917-1929, the United States in no way shrunk from taking such similar risks when it saved Italy, Serbia, Greece, Liberia and Costa

Rica with U.S. loans.

If the signs do not prove deceptive, then the question of an American loan to Russia guaranteed by the state will enter a new stage with the recognition of the Soviet Union. Following such a loan, the German American competition for the Russian market would intensify. Such competition however extends only to those areas in which German exports cut into the American exports. Electrical fittings and machine industries belong first and foremost to this category. Former American exports to Russia were composed for the most part of product groups in which German export industry rarely competes. For the time being it is enormous farm machinery that, owing to similar large acreages as in America, can be used in Russia. In the future, it will be tractors, somewhat later automobiles and lastly, typewriters and calculating machines. Appropriate cooperation should enable the peaceful German-American trade on the Russian market.

Wherein then reside the difficulties that still prevent a German-American friendship and international cooperation? The problem is not in the area of trade. It is not in the area of foreign policy either. If German-American relations are not as friendly currently as they might be, it lies essentially in a critical American attitude towards the internal political developments in Germany. But the problems should not be overestimated. Skillful propaganda, always ready to promote an anti-German spirit, has been used against us. The American administration has up till now nevertheless applied an appropriate brake. It is quite inconceivable that America will enter into a crusade because of our Jewish problem. According to reports, edited in New York, one should not mix New York up with the rest of America. Americans vigorously defend themselves against this mistake. Although New York's Jewish population of one third is the largest percentage of any world capital, the political influence of New York City is by no means as powerful as is sometimes assumed in Germany. Furthermore, Jewish actions in Washington have not been impressive and do not account for the mood across the country.

The assessment of church-related questions, however, is considerably more serious. Given the unusual power of the Protestant denominations in the United States, the interest directed towards German church-political developments should under no circumstances be underestimated.

Finally, after a long period of vacancies in the American embassy in Berlin, these will soon be occupied following a reshuffling in the other European capitals. It means that there will no longer be obstacles on the path toward the restoration of normal relations between the United States and Germany. Much will depend on the personality of the new ambassador to Germany as well as on the welcome he will receive in Berlin whether the German-American friendship can become more amiable in the coming years.

December 19, 1933.

Honorable William E. Dodd,
Ambassador of the United States,
Berlin, Germany.

My dear Dodd:

I shall be very grateful if you
will give the inclosed to Dr. Helmut
Magers.

It was very good of you to write
the preface, and I appreciate it.

As ever yours,

Franklin D. Roosevelt

The White House

1933

December 19, 1933.

Dr. Helmut Hagers,
c/o Honorable William E. Dodd,
Berlin, Germany.

My dear Dr. Hagers:

I want to send you my thanks for
the copy of your little book about me
and the "New Deal". Though, as you
know, I went to school in Germany
and could speak German with considerable
fluency at one time, I am reading
your book not only with great interest
but because it will help my German.

Very sincerely yours,

Franklin D Roosevelt

The White House

1933